ALSO BY WILLIAM HEYEN

Depth of Field (1970)
Noise in the Trees: Poems and a Memoir (1974)
The Swastika Poems (1977)

William Heyen

THE VANGUARD PRESS, INC.   NEW YORK

Long Island Light

POEMS AND A MEMOIR

Many of the poems collected here first appeared in the following publications, to whose editors grateful acknowledgment is made: *The American Review* ("The Pigeons"); *Ann Arbor Review* ("Bailing," "Afternoon," "Man of the Sea," "The Traffic"); *The Back Door* ("A Tour on the Prairies"); *Four Quarters* ("Pet's Death," "The Nesconset Crickets"); *The Georgia Review* ("This Father of Mine," "The Heart," "Brockport, New York: Beginning with 'And' "); *The Iowa Review* ("The Ewe"); *Ironwood* (Part II of "The Elm's Home"); *The Long Pond Review* ("The Witch"); *Modern Poetry Studies* ("Refrain"); *New Generation: Poetry* ("The Founding"); *The New Yorker* ("Clamming at St. James Harbor," "Four Songs," Part I of "The Elm's Home"); *The Ohio Review* ("Dog Sacrifice at Lake Ronkonkoma," "Cow, Willow, Skull, Cowbell," "The Lamb," "Candling," "Witness," "Wenzel"); *Poetry Northwest* ("My Deer"); *Poetry* ("The Snapper," "The Crow," "Anthem," "The Swan," "The Trail Beside the River Platte," "The Return," "Fires"); *Prairie Schooner* ("Crabbing at St. James Harbor," "Where It Began," "Worming at Short Beach," "The Mill"); *Prism International* ("Legend of the Tree at the Center of the World"); *Rapport* ("The Carrie White Auction at Brockport, May 1974"); *Service-berry* ("The Language"); *The Southern Review* ("The Cat," "Maple and Starlings," "The River"); *Strivers' Row* ("Oak Autumn," "Oak Spring"); *Sycamore* ("For the Year 2500," Part V of "The Elm's Home"); *Thistle* ("The Circle," "Bus Trip"); *The University of Windsor Review* ("Of Gatsby"); *Vanderbilt Poetry Review* ("Tonging at St. James Harbor," "This Island"); *Western Humanities Review* ("Texts," "The Odor of Pear").

"Invocation" and "The Crane at Gibbs Pond" first appeared in *From This Book of Praise*, edited by Vince Clemente (Street Press, 1978), as did section XXVII of "Noise in the Trees: A Memoir." Sections II–XIII of the memoir first appeared in *Prose*, sections XIV–XV, XVII–XVIII, and XX–XXI in *Strivers' Row*. Section XXVI was first published as a broadside called *The Pearl* by Patti and Tony Petrosky at their Slow Loris Press, which also published a broadside of "The Fireman Next Door." Section XXIX first appeared in *West Hills Review*. Special thanks to Cis and Ernie Stefanik of Rook Press who first published "Mermaid," "Pickerel," and "Dusk" as broadsides, and *Cardinals/The Cardinal* and *Son Dream/Daughter Dream,* two pamphlets.

The author also wishes to thank the State University of New York Research Foundation and the John Simon Guggenheim Memorial Foundation for fellowships during which parts of this book were written.

For Han, my wife,
and for Bill and Kristen,
our children

And all the uses of nature admit of being summed into one, which yields the activity of man an infinite scope. Through all its kingdoms, to the suburbs and outskirts of things, it is faithful to the cause whence it had its origin.

—EMERSON

It was the first time in my life I ever understood something, and I am far from sure now that I can put down what I understood and felt that night—I mean something about the connection between certain people and the earth.

—SHERWOOD ANDERSON

Contents

I

I

The Nesconset Crickets

Either the crickets stopped,
or I fell asleep as they kept on.

But sometimes I'd count their song
all night, when I couldn't sleep,

or dreamed I couldn't sleep, or dreamed
from under grass that I helped them sing.

Invocation

Outside our bedroom window
a nightshift of crickets works hard in the heavy dark.
To lie awake is to live,
to sleep is to die, I think, as I open and close my eyes.

A crescent, your cheekbone, floats real
as the pale moon beside me—
is this the secret, then? Is this the love
I could once only imagine?

In the air of the night of this room,
I breathe your breath, deeply, slowly.
I am drifting back, into your body, drifting
back, into your body.

Where It Began

A few tides each summer
the soft skulls of jellyfish,
their tendons filtering the green water,
drift by thousands close to the Sound's shores.

A few tides each summer
spawns of sandworms choke the Sound,
pale blue, translucent, edged with blood,
bits of vein in the green water.

Worming at Short Beach

At Short Beach, reaching
  almost to the horizon, successions
    of sandbars lay bared

to the low tide, the furthest,
  toward which I walked
    over the wormgrounds,

toward which I waded
  through shallow sluices of channel,
    almost indistinct, and now blurred,

a small island of the mind
  I've tried to touch,
    define, and hold.

But I remember, as gulls worked
  the water's edge, ripped
    hermits from houses of shell,

or in my wake split
  the razors I threw aside,
    I remember, my back against

the sun's blaze, worming that far bar,
  forking close to clumps of sawgrass,
    turning the wet sand over,

6

breaking the worms' domains
   open to the dark sheen
      of my shadow.

My fork rasped against
   the shells of softclams
      that sprayed small geysers

as I dug, and the wind
   was a thin whisper of scythes
      over the waves. And now,

all this from a long time ago
   is almost lost
      and goes nowhere, except deeper,

year by year. But this was the way,
   when I worked that far bar,
      the light fell: the sandworms

were blood-red in my shadow,
   as I forked them
      into my shadow.

The Mill

Over the harbor at St. James
a windmill lifted its oars to the sun,
but the sun cast the mill,
trunk and branches, down again
in shadow against the waves,
or, when the water was windless as glass,
mirrored the mill there.

Those breathless days, I'd clam
in the mill's image, each of its lines clear,
until I'd rake, or jerk the floating bushel.
The mill would break,
but reassemble, shingle by shingle.
Mine and the mill's form
were written in water.

Crabbing at St. James Harbor

Gulls hover against
an invisible wind,
but the mill's oars
are still,
rusted dead by centuries
of salt air.

I've been here before,
kneeling on the sand,
skewering minnows
to lengths of wire.

One foot in this, one
in the other life,
I push offshore,
power between the rows of buoys
to the smooth water over
the mudhole at the center
of the harbor,

cut the motor,
drop anchor
to crab.

The circles of minnows
touch bottom.

I've been here before,
and beyond, past
the harbor's mouth,
toward where the water falls, past
what it is I'm waiting for.

A line throbs
against my fingers. A crab,
treading a floor no man
can walk upon, tries
to pull away.
I draw him toward me, wanting,
again, to live among the living.

Clamming at St. James Harbor

I

As I dragged the bullrake belted at my waist,
backed away, my weight against the chain,
my arms hauling at the crossbars,
and brought the basket up

filled with waterlogged driftwood, starfish,
stones, spidercrabs, snails, shells,
and sorted out the few clams
big enough to keep,

flounders scribbled ahead of their mud wakes,
schools of transparent minnows dotted
and dashed codes against my legs,
young eels kissed my sneakers

with words: this you shall always remember.
This water is the true blood, this
shore is the true body, this
sky the incarnate light.

II

Now, years later, perhaps walking, or reading,
or talking to someone I've long loved,
I leave my self to kneel
at my own grave.

I kneel in a flat of the harbor at low tide, beside
a trench I've raked, facing the mill's oars
that now whirl down a lattice
of sun and shadow.

I hold relics in my arms: the jeweled claws of crabs,
strands of seaweed shining like saints' hair,
skates' eggs like black scarabs,
clamshells white as time's

waters could wash them. Each time now I kneel longer,
until the tide shall turn, the sun's red blade
drop, gulls fall from the night's tree
to my eyes like dark leaves.

This Island

Low tides, early mornings,
I'd walk the mud flats for nothing,
saying, as reeds bowed, straightened,
and bowed again in the brine wind,
or an eel or flounder startled
a cloudy trail through low water,
know you have forever, now,
know you have forever.

The Sound fallen back, this Island
risen, I kneel, touch my head
like a reed to the mud home of the crab,
wash my face in a gull's shadow,
knowing I have forever, now,
knowing I have forever.

Bailing

The brine mist lifts.
Heat waves rise from the sand
and sandbars from the waves.
The storm is over.

In the harbor
our small boats
are still swamped,
their anchor ropes

twisted together as a reel's
backlash. The sun's
steady rhythms beat
on our backs as we bail.

If the channel's buoys
broke from their chains
and swept out to the Sound,
it doesn't matter. For now,

we've lost desire
for the deep water.
Yesterday, the storm. Today, bailing
in the sun and salt air.

Afternoon

The storm is over:
the brine mist lifts;
the harbor's dark water begins to clear;

clams rise in their beds, some
to seine the settling mud, some
to the embrace of starfish;

crabs tear the dazed and dead;
eels prowl for uprooted bloodworms;
horseshoes, dragging their daggers
back to shore, scar the mud floor;

gulls scree, dive, rise
with minnows that drip light
and flash in their beaks as they fly.

The storm is over;
the sun burns at white heat;
by noon, the mill has swallowed

its own shadow; by four, its oars
stretch darkness back across the harbor.
The storm is over:
tomorrow, we'll fish the deep water.

Tonging at St. James Harbor

I
Late fall, because the water bit,
was time to drive
that dead-end dirt road
to nowhere,
to nose my car
against a bank of sawgrass,
to walk that shell and fishbone path
winding down to the harbor
where my rowboat rose
on the sweet mud
of low tide;
was time to muscle against
the brine wind, to stand
over the boat's side;
was time to tong.

II
Those were late falls,
and long ago,
but the twenty-foot poles
still slide
down my shadow.
I still spread my arms wide
as a martyred saint's,
and bring them together
with nails in my wrists

and whips at my shoulders,
still feel those tongs scissor
and fall, still claw
that bottom of weed and shell
that yielded bushel
after bushel.

III
I've said this so often,
but have said nothing,
but there's still more:
except for gulls
that floated like prayers of white paper;
except for billions of lives
beating in their shells, sheathes, and scales
beneath me, I worked alone.
I rocked those waves alone.
And later, packing chowders
back along the same path where none
but stars and white wild roses held
the evening air,
I knew that everything I'd ever bless, or be,
would come to this.

IV
I warned you:
now,
in my loneliness,
be with me

as I tong.
Are we the last
to hear it?
That beauty disappears,
but lives,
if this is the pulse
of waves,
if this is the Island's vast
soft wingbeat and heartbeat,
if ours is the only
abiding love.

Legend of the Tree at the Center of the World

Blizzard. The greak oak's roots
snapped from sand.
Wind blew it across the Lake Ronkonkoma ice
where, between shores, it settled, like a forest.

The next was a bell-clear morning:
Sun glittered its limbs until
green leaves appeared from Never.
Then the lake's roof fell.

All night the water swirled. Gods
battled beneath the ice. Moon
plunged near and shook loose showers
of arrows. That morning was the first Spring.

Dog Sacrifice at Lake Ronkonkoma

Now spears lift them by their ribs
over the black water to heaven.
Now they are almost dead.
Their eyes blaze in the moonlight,

as, all dark long,
the sacred lake laps shore
with syllables of approaching spring.
Men listen, the dogs stare and die, until,

Ronkonkoma, its curves a skull,
dreaming in its own bottomless bed,
fills with the first light of morning,
and the sun rises, clothed in the dogs' blood.

The Founding

On the Island's South Shore
clams and oysters were dredged up,
buried alive under mounds of dirt,
left to decay, uncovered,
their bodies scraped from their shells.

This blue-black money touched
the whole country.
On the Pacific Coast
John Jacob Astor traded whole cartloads
and built an empire.

The whole country was touched
with this money, which carried disease,
which smelled like dead fish,
which men weighed and kissed,
by candlelight, in their dark cellars.

Smith's Ride

(In 1660 the Nissequogue Indians of Long Island
gave Richard Smith, in exchange for trinkets and
cattle and guns, as much land as he could encircle
between sunrise and sunset, riding bareback on a
bull. The path Smith and his bull broke marks the
present boundaries of Smithtown Township.)

I

Every Halloween the balls
of Smith's bronze bull are painted gold,
its cock sheathed with prophylactics.
Then how to reach out and touch

you, and Smith, with Smith's story? Still,
he says *yes*, smacks his broken bull
on its shoulder, which levels high as his,
and in whose eyes the red sun rises,

now, over the windless darkness
of trees, toward noon,
when he had better be outward and near
swinging back, for evening

still falls early, spring's flowers fold
against the wet cold early,
morning glories slow and sleep already,
and the dew dries.

II

Then his will be,
and in his way: he mounts,
turns the bull toward woods,
now enters a white gloom where birches clump,

tells himself to ride clear
of where the land falls into ferns,
into false lily of the valley,
where the bull's hoofs plash and churn leaves,

and the wet worsens. Smith leans over
the wide horns, marks the land's rise to his right,
landmarks a maple, arcs part
of his circle to its base. *Yes,*

and the leaves catch more glitter,
the Indian dead waken
in Smith's and the bull's rush: now he owns
a stream edged in cattails; now, a dogwood hill.

III

Each new leaf uncurls, fills with light,
but brush thickens, forces
one of the long halters and walks,
the bull stepping in Smith's steps, closing

its eyes against the bramble and thorn
of Smith's backlash. They rest:

the Island listens, and to what?
Even the jays are silent as blue flowers,

squirrels freeze against their bark,
a brown bear licks light
from a tree's trunk and fades away
to nowhere. This Smith driving back

toward his beginning—what does he know?
We walk swamps of pavement
where he walked the bull to his will.
He circles, drives, swings wide.

IV

So Smith hunches forward and backward
to ease his back, drives on,
breaks brush, breaks into clearings
where dead fires blacken the ground,

or deer browse, or creeks cut.
And the land listens, and waits.
He thinks: this is the noose, the necklace,
the shape of my desire, the loose circle

of the New World's gift, the island
within an island, the brain's skull,
the marrow's bone, the eye's socket,
the foot's boot. He stops for meat,

24

bread, a goatskin of milk, wipes his mouth,
kisses his hand to the woods,
which breathes and waits, catches,
and begins to repeat the wind.

V

The bull's back sweats, and bareback the terms
of Smith's barter. He traps his hands
in his bull's hide, or holds to horn, steers
by main strength in the maize light,

in the honey light half the world's
and its plunging sun, half
Smith's own dazed brain's. But he keeps on,
for the ships' terror, the vermin,

scurvy, boils, rashes, for the Island's
wolves, storms, howls, graves
dug in deep snow. And for its gulls
that wing low and white over the harbor's

calm, out to the sea's spray
and curl where, under the whitecaps,
blue crabs wait for bushels and fire,
fish swarm, clams seed and seine the tides.

VI

So Smith hunches forward and backward
over the bull's back, drives on,
dreams the New World's gifts.
The bull's back sweats blood

from the whipping brush, gnats gather
to a gold haze in the fading light, cobwebs
glitter like gilt threads, his hands
wear the bull's horns to a shine. This

Smith—what could he know? Now
only the ghost of a wind whispers
where no trees stand, snowplows
scrape sparks from the roads

where he rode hellbent.
His graveyard flashes with neon flowers.
We witness and wait.
His will be.

VII

Where he began
his wife and children wait.
His ride done and the last sun touching
the woman's white skirt, he swings down,

embraces her, says, perhaps:
This is our land. The forest

falls into darkness around them, the bull
drops his head to the wet grass. Time leafs

and leaves them, shadows in a clearing,
forever: the woman, the rider
whose arm she holds, the sons
who will descend here,

and the bull, whose spirit is metal,
who now stares at the traffic below him,
these cars that climb the hill like deer,
trucks that lurch his wilderness like bear.

Texts

Twain meant that as Huck drifted
toward Jackson's Island
he was already dead.
He'd killed a pig
and splashed its blood around
and stuck his hair to an ax
for Pap to find. And later,
hiding near shore,
hidden by brush and the thick fog
of a dream, he heard, between
cannon thumps and rushes of wind,
voices he knew from the old life,
and watched loaves of bread
weighted with quicksilver
float by to find him.
But Twain meant that by this time

Huck was already dead,
and this island, island of dream,
dark, heavy-timbered,
"like a steamboat," he says,
"like a steamboat without any lights,"
this island toward which,
already dead, Huck drifted,
this island that seemed,
like Fulton's ships on the Hudson,
to be driving upriver,
is prophecy, this

is the country, this has something
to do with sadness, this
is what he saw, this
is what he knew, this
dark island completes the story.

His beginning exists in his end,
his end in his beginning,
for Huck knew what was ahead:
the machine, a love
to accept and despair of.
In the beginning,
before he lived or chose to,
the machine rose up
from the fog, the steamboat
dividing the river, and the cities
were always there
under the dark water,
and where men settled
wheat waved golden in the sun,
threshers rose up from the soil,
and all the old sins

filled the sails of ships
that first drove homeward
to America. And Twain knew,
and Dreiser, and fated Hart Crane,
and Faulkner, whose Ike watched
the two-toed bear older
than legend, the great "locomotive-
like shape," appear and disappear

like a whale in its swirl;
and Ben, the locomotive, slain,
the engine rounds the bend
of the wilderness again, where
it was born. In his beginning
and in his end, in his dream
and his dream's end,
the land smells of metal.

To a Warplane

As you wait in your hidden hangar,
being of such sleek beauty,
now bending even the faint moonlight
gleaming along your body

into the nightstreak of rockets,
hundred-million dollar angel,
nuclear deliverer,
swept-wing, black-silver metrical

veined and blooded with secret
electronic and hydraulic systems,
fierce and lovely essence, American
numina of soft cockpit leather, guardian

of the deadly flame and of the power,
thee, for my recitative, thee.

The Traffic

Red lights pulse and weave in
toward an accident ahead.
Trying to leave Smithtown,
I'm stopped dead,

here, where Whitman trooped
to tally the eighth-month flowers' bloom.
Diesels jam their bumpers together in a long line,
gas and rubber heat wafts in like soup.

A truck's exhaust curves up beside me
like a swan's neck. I sigh,
make a mistake, and breathe deep.
Concrete, signs, and cars cloud:

Lilacs utter their heart-shaped leaves,
locusts spell their shade. The Jericho's air
creaks with cartwheels, a carriage
moves with the certainty of mirage.

The Widow Blydenburgh flows to church,
stoops to admire an iris, and to smell.
A pigeon bends the slim branch of a birch.
The Widow plucks the iris for her Bible.

Horns soon blare me out of this.
Trailing a plume of smoke,
the trucker grunts his rig ahead.
I accelerate past a cop

directing traffic around the wreck.
He asks if I'm all right. I nod
and close the lane. Glass sparkles,
a splash of blood still shines

on the pavement, and time's itself again.
Pressed against the porch of Whitman's school,
the Dairy Freeze is booming, winks
its windows tinted green, and cool.

The Trail beside the River Platte

He saw, abandoned to the sand,
"claw-footed tables, once well waxed
and rubbed, or massive bureaus
of carved oak," now blistered,

sun-scorched, and warped.
So, the Ogillallah lived
as they had lived, rode
their ponies where the plains

were still humped black with buffalo—
enough, it seemed,
for the whole country
to feast on tongues, forever.

But the herds, of course, were doomed,
and the "large wandering communities"
that followed them would follow them
to nowhere. Parkman remembered

a day when innumerable animals thundered
into a ravine:
"Hoofs were jerked upwards," he said,
"tails flourished

in the air, and amid a cloud
of dust, the buffalo seemed
to sink into the earth
before me."

The Pigeons

Audubon watched the flocks beat by for days,
and tried, but could not count them:
their dung fell "like melting flakes of snow,"
the air buzzed until he lost his senses.

He heard, he said, their *coo-coo*
and *kee-kee* when they courted, and saw trees
of hundreds of nests, each cradling two
"broadly elliptical pure white eggs."

Over mast, they swept in "rich deep purple
circles," then roosted so thick that high limbs
cracked, and the pigeons avalanched
down the boughs, and had not room to fly,

and died by thousands. Kentucky farmers
fed their hogs on birds
knocked out of the air with poles. No net, stone,
arrow, or bullet could miss one,

so horses drew wagons of them,
and schooners sailed cargoes of them,
and locomotives pulled freight cars of them
to the cities where they sold for one cent each.

When you touched one, its soft
feathers fell away as easily as a puff
of dandelion seeds, and its delicate breast-
bone seemed to return the pulse of your thumb.

Cardinals

When I was a kid I watched
Wenzel shoot them out of his appletrees,
those beautiful cardinals,
the males brighter than their mates,
and better targets.

All the summer's bees
tunnelled those bodies.
The redbirds' breastbones hummed,
the bees were that busy
among the windfalls.

One female lay eye-
high in a branch
as though alive,
though her eyes were closed.
When I walked into the tree,

when, with my thumb,
I touched her soft head-
feathers, a cap of skin
skimmed from her skull,
and I was happy.

When you and I hear
a call along the air,
one that is not pretty, that
does not trill or lilt,
should we trace it and kill it?

The Cardinal

They were wild and far away
until he killed them.
You understand:
I wanted to hold them still,
see them clearly.

For a second her skull,
the curved blue-white blunt
end of an egg, or eye,
met the sun. Then
blood washed in.

Should I hold her here, red
feather by gray feather, thumb
open her blood-washed eye again,
listen to bee-song under her beak,
hum her other visceral melodies?

I've asked you to help me, to share,
to touch her. Tell me,
as you rub these lines with your thumb,
is this the same, or
was that a life ago?

She was only one cardinal.
We didn't kill her,
but there were others.
Now, if we must have her,
we must have her here.

Pickerel

Green body flowing yellow,
horizontal flame
lit under padshadow,
among bending lily stems,

gills fanning
rings, ripples, water-
lights—now its pond
is dead.   How many years?

My eyes its amber
to hold it.   It disappeared,
but hovers,
here.

The Crane at Gibbs Pond
(for my mother)

The boy stood by the darkening pond
watching the other shore.
Against pines,
a ghostly crane floated
from side to side,
crooning.   Maybe
its mate had drowned.   Maybe
its song lamented
the failing sun.   Maybe
its plaint was joy,
the heart-stricken praise
for its place of perfect loneliness.   Maybe,
hearing its own echoing,
taking its own phantom gliding
the sky mirror of the pond
for its lost mother in her other world,
it tried to reach her
in the only way it could.   Maybe,
as night diminished
all but the pond's black radiance,
the boy standing there
knew he would some day sing
of the crane, the crane's song,
and the soulful water.

This Father Of Mine

*I want to show you something
very beautiful,* I say to my father
in this dream.   We are walking
a tar road in Nesconset

around a slow bend
I still remember
where elms rose up
every evening of every summer

into great forests of darkness,
and blue-black birds swept
from one branch to another.
I want to show you something

very beautiful, I say, and take him
by his hand that never held
a book, his palm hardened
by boards and the handles

of a hundred hammers.
I notice sawdust
in the hair on his forearm.
I want to show you something

very beautiful.   Now,
past the road's pebble and sand shoulder,

we step into oakbrush
where a path winds downward

to a pond I still remember.
In this dream the pond,
as it once was, is lipped
by ferns mirroring themselves

in green triangles
all along its edge.
On the far shore
a crane beats up out of the water,

curves over the trees,
hangs suspended
on its white wings
as though it were the white moon climbing

motionless in time
for as long as we stare.   But
*I want to show you something
very beautiful*, I say to him,

and now, somehow, at the end
of the path of this dream,
we are barefoot, wading out
to knee-high water where

the pond's bottom disappears
into a depth I still remember.

There, I say to him,
and point down.   But

from his pocket
he takes a handkerchief,
and stands, this father of mine,
knee-high in water in no hurry

wiping his glasses.
Over the far shore
the white crane still flies
to nowhere, motionless

as the white moon.   But
there, I say, and point down, and now, at last,
we are looking down again
into the dream together,

into the pond's deepest beginnings,
into the place I remember
where elms rise toward surface
from the black water, from

thousands of fathoms, each leaf
distinct, each trunk furrowed
black and deep as a field
of plowed loam.   *There:*

fish swim in the branches and bark valleys,
blue-black carp that vanish

and appear, and vanish again,
and appear.   Their gills

glow red, their tails seem
to spray wakes of pale
yellow arcs as the fish vanish,
and appear, and vanish again, and appear.

Yes, he says, *yes*, and now
as though from his one word
spoken into the darkness of this dream,
the carp scatter

downward and outward
forever.   And now that I have held
our two worlds together
for as long as this, the day,

in the whitest light we have ever seen,
rises from the bottom of the water through the elms.
It is over, I think,
though I almost remember

that we hold hands again,
and talk for the first time,
and walk toward home,
which is far away.

Anthem

I descended once
    into madness where
        a bell does swing above its bell-rope,

the spinal column,
    a low lead reverberation,
        the struck sound spaced vertebrae apart.

My carpenter father's gluepot filled,
    again, with sawdust.
        Broken, bearing his pockets'

emptiness behind his eyes,
    he washed his hands in our narrow kitchen,
        my mother screaming, "Where's our money,

where's our money?" I watched them
    slam themselves into their rusted Ford
        and drive away.   Then

that bell began.   Was it real?   Had its waves
    carried to our lawn
        from miles away where,

betrayed, dead, my Jesus lay suspended
    in robes of stained glass, but about to rise
        into the sun's rays?

But this was not my church:
　　I listened to the bell
　　　　toll syllables of madness while

the real sun's spectrum and glisten
　　rushed out of a huge backyard elm
　　　　like a sunburst in reverse.

I remember running with the bell
　　into the back woods—
　　　　brush-slash and blood until

all color returned to the world.
　　That bell diminished,
　　　　and I who had heard its call to darkness,

the death knell, had entered the vacuum
　　that drew all light at mid-day
　　　　out of the great tree,

I who had found that country
　　where my parents sang
　　　　"Give us money, money, money,

or give us death, O America,"
　　walked out of the woods as they died.

Of Gatsby

Night, "wings beating in the trees."
Now Nick sees he isn't alone:
fifty feet away his neighbor trembles
and stretches his arms out toward the bay:
a green light shines over
the Island's mysterious water
like a mirage of emerald fire.
But Gatsby cannot be approached.
Soon, as though he were never there,
Gatsby is gone.

But in his deepest scene Gatsby decides
to name his name.
He taps at Nick's door in the rain
until it opens wider
than his whole life can bear.
After an impossible hello again
to the golden girl of his own composition,
he leans against a mantle, almost
knocking a dead clock to the floor.
Fitzgerald knew that this was time
for tears: Gatsby will take her home,
their hearts will begin to kindle,
she'll cry into a pile of his shirts.

In the raw sunlight when the year
turned for one last season
to gray woodsmoke and ashes,

Gatsby's blood touched the water red.
Nick returned to stocks and bonds,
and she, since she could not be there
to save the forsaken dreamer
from his dream, just disappeared.
Only we are left
to drive his opulent driveway once or twice,
to know his house like no one else.

The Fireman Next Door

I

Somewhere,
beyond his Dalmatian's high-pitched ear,
a fire roars,
a school or mansion burns,
and forever.
He feels it in his bones,
and all night handles axes, ladders,
streams of water,
women in boots, in nightgowns.

But the edges of his dreams waver.
Red engines burn rubber
on their way home.
His blood falls with the wail of sirens.

II

Morning:
the sun rises in a psalm of flame.
He wakes to his alarm,
shaves and dresses
for the long day ahead
of mopping floors and pushing a broom.
His wife fries eggs and nods
at the news
of last night's meeting.

When he leaves home
she'll sigh and find her solace back in bed,
dreaming of the new hose
that sprays foam.

III

Taking a bus,
or packed in a rattle of trains,
or driving to work,
we all cry out as the day begins:
Lord, hear us,
we've paid plenty for our sins.
Simple is the world, and simple
our desire:
send my neighbor the fire

he yearns for, his wife the deep dream
of meaning.
We'll need a world where flame rains down
to kiss us, where water burns.

Landscapes

I

Yanking roots,
tractors drag chains that clank
like lead coins. Bulldozers mine the woods.

We say:
what stories our redwood benches
could tell, our picnic tables, our knickknack shelves.

In winter,
windows of ice scrape over
logs floating in swimming pools like coffins.

Across the Island,
the shadows of its trees
strain to touch their long fingers together

above those yards
where only the dead gather.

II

Smith's bull still
stares beyond the dark maples,
but we have rushed this far this fast: a bison,

bearded, shagged,
looks out through bars
on a shopping center's grand opening.

Cages line
a flat-bed truck. Come, see
a skunk, an eagle, a snake, a calf with five legs.

III

On the Jericho
that April morning

one black Cadillac
pulled beside another

and sprayed it with lead.
Also the driver.

The papers said
the Island was a good spot

for rub-outs.
I heard the shots

while weeding a bed of hyacinths
lately sprung

from the rich loam.
Their perfume

touched the air
as the assassins headed home.

You always remember
what you were doing.

The Witch

I

Witch hazel waves its yellow flowers, moths
perish in the oval of my lantern.
As fast as the thick brush allows
I follow, into the glades
of darkness,

where the witch flutters, now
fading, folding her wings to a deadfall, now
rising from tree to tree.   Leaves
rush in her wind

as she glides, silhouette,
through branches, into
hollows of the sky.

She floats down.   Ferns,
still green in their black sheen,
sway.   She passes,
as though the wind were animal,
and took her form.

My rifle gleams,
its barrel, the polished wood
of its stock.

The wet brush
whips my face to tears.

II

Each year we hear less.
She is among the last,
and is deranged, leaving the forest, crying
was, was, over the village
as we sleep.

The Book says
burn out her eyes,
the invisible world's wonders.

We've become afraid
for our children, remember the stories,
the children following, never
to return.

Our wives dream of her whose wings
brush them in their sleep.
Our guns lean in their corners, pointing
at the witch.

III

This is the night of the witch.
This is the night the witch must die.
The moon falls behind rainclouds.
My dogs howl and drag me ahead.
Brush swallows my path.

The witch rises, seems,
far ahead, over the marshland,
to pulse white.   Blood
beats in my ears.   Tonight
I'll follow her, carry her back,
black feathers, bones, beak,
the strip of red fur
that curls in the curve of her neck.

All night the steeples' bells
will toll the death of the witch.
All night the bellropes will writhe.

IV

The Book says
track the witch, drive
arrows or bullets through her, mark
her fall, do not lose her, cut out her eyes,
crush them, burn them, chop
her wings and legs from her body, bury her
in a pit of lime, build a fire
above her grave.

The Book says
blessed be her killers.

The Book says
it is witch that trembles

under the surface of dark water,
witch that skids the wind,
deadfall and ascension,
witch that gapes the mouths of flowers.

V

I move closer.
The witch seems to wear
vestments of pewter, hovers
over the marsh.   Now she
settles, cries, like an owl, *you, you.*

I crash through the thick brush.
The mesh floor of the marsh
gurgles, bullfrogs pray
to their crane king,
rain begins
falling, the leaves
spit.   Now
she sees me, turns
toward me, herself
the only soft light of the darkness,
her eyes embers.

I am close enough, fire,
and the witch rises, shrieks
never, floats over the trees,
over my head.

I have been here before.
All my lives
the witch has escaped me.

VI

This was a long time ago.
I read The Book and rock.
I find myself wondering,
what is it I've hunted?—

but know she is not the hag
of brooms and castles, of toads and cauldrons.
She is not the crone of still waters and mirrors.
She is not the witch of reflection.

This was a long time ago.
I rock and watch the fire.
I find myself wondering,
when will the covenant be broken?—

but, even now, across this Island the same
crickets scrape in the nightwind, the same
lights still glow over the marshland, the same
witch remembers my name.

My Deer

I

As the Island was falling
I was drawing on the walls of the cave.
I've lived here since the first tremors.

Trees fell across the cave's mouth.
My charcoal deer were flushed green.
Light rippled their flanks like water.

The wind rose and opened the eye of the cave.
Light shone orange through the dust.
My deer pawed the flames.

When the Island fell I searched
for my deer by the sparks of stones.
I lie here alone in the dark.

II

I am glad of that other life,
the charcoal I rubbed on the cave's walls,
my deer that moved with the sun
before the Island fell.

Even though the weather is over,
the rain's hoofs clatter.
Even in the cave's dark
the trees' antlers click together.

This is my sleep and a dream,
or my first awakening, or both.
I am glad of my deer.
The dark has many doors.

III

I have heard, lying here beyond
measurements of time, the Sound

swelling above this chamber, seeping
down. The cave's roof weeps

cones, horns of lime.
Its floor grows stone columns.

When I lost my eyes I began
to see. Now I am pure, white bone,

fused to the cave's floor.
Blind bats dip and skitter

down from their ledges, where
clouds of white mist gather.

IV

The mist rolls down.
Stone ferns bloom white
on the cave's floor.

My deer walk in woodsmoke,
sip the edges of dark pools.
Vapor rises from fur.

One buck of light moves near,
licks my ribs from the floor
with his warm tongue.
I have nothing to forgive.
I am glad of my deer,
the life I lived, and live.

V

This bodiless life, this presence—
how have I stayed this long
in the deer light of earth,
once my body's home?

Be with me, far past those old desires.
Be with me: remember the dead
luminous Island
and its holy air.

You—I can see you now, even hear
your heartbeat beating near.
Be with me,
as I become my deer.

For The Year 2500

In Long Island's sand, my fingers
   found this talisman,
this small tri-
   angular deer skull
      to hold to your eye.

Within its milky glow
   against the sun, notice
the thin brainpan's curved
   veins of whiter bone, the white
      wheel spokes, the radiant

creation, the crystalline-based
   star-pattern born
in the Word, in water, in sperm.
   Every skull holds our sun's first fires.
      Your dead Lord lives at the wheel's hub.

II

Noise in the Trees: A Memoir

> *I called to my boy, bidding him go out and
> see what noise this could be. The boy said:
> "The moon and stars are shining; the Milky
> Way glitters in the sky. Nowhere is there any
> noise of men. The noise must be in the trees."*
>
> Ou-Yang Hsui

I

I have not walked this way for a long time, but I am not
surprised to find myself walking here.

I have not, I consider, walked this way for ten years. The
shops in St. James have not changed, and the elms, at this
time just before evening sets in, still throw a weak shade on
the sidewalk.

The air is cool. It is spring. I am wearing my too-baggy
black pants and I have the uncomfortable feeling that my
shoelaces are untied or not tied tightly enough. My walk is
awkward.

There are no cars on the street or people on the side-
walks. I tighten my belt a notch and hitch up my pants. My
undershirt keeps pulling up, pulling my shirt out of my
pants.

In front of her father's shop on the corner, his barberpole,
already dimly lit against the evening, spirals its red and
white stripes. Moths batter its glass cylinder. We must re-
ceive the light, I say to myself, we must not attack.

I see myself in one of the shop's windows, and see myself

again in the mirror behind the cash register between the chairs. He would say I needed a haircut.

His register gleams softly, silver and black. I wonder if what she told me is true: that each day Gregersen descends with his proceeds to his cellar to hide the money in a tin can behind a loose cement block.

I have lost my shoes. I am obsessed with the idea that I have lost my shoes, that they must be somewhere in the Gregersens' apartment behind the shop. They have no right to my shoes. I must get them back. I move around the corner and enter their garage. They still have the green Oldsmobile. I open the door of their car that leads to their kitchen. Remembering that there are three steps up, I am careful.

Night has fallen. I stand in their kitchen and can hear crickets singing from under the stones of the neat flowerbeds outside. I remember passing a florist's shop down the street. Only calendars gathered dust on the display shelves in its window, their monthly flowers flat and dirty in the dull light.

I make my way to her room. She is asleep on a dark blue bedspread that drapes to the floor. Her face is turned to the wall. Somewhere in the house water trickles in the plumbing.

I can just see the heels of my shoes jutting out from under her bed. As I reach for them she turns over, her hair yellow in the soft light. Pretending I do not know that she sees me, wondering if she will give me away, I pick up my shoes and leave.

I am outside, cutting across their lawn, my shoes still in my hands. The grass is wet. I am almost to the row of poplars that lines the sidewalk when the screen door opens and Gregersen shouts:

. . . I told you never, you, never to bring my daughter

home this late. I warned you. I've called the police. Who do you think you are?

The door slams. Shutters on an upstairs window open and Karen leans out. She is wearing a white blouse. I am glad it is dark. My hair is too long and my pants are baggy. She slams the shutters.

. . . Karen, don't, I say.

She opens the screen door. She points a finger and shouts at me.

. . . I told you it was all over I told you. What did you think? Leave me alone stay away. . . .

My son is with me. It is too damp here for him. I slip my shoes over my wet socks and, without bothering to tie them, lift him up. We brush through the poplars into the deep shade of the elms over the sidewalk. I walk toward home as fast as I can.

II

She was, is, all my dark girls. And the land at last encircled by Smith and his bull on a sunfall more than three centuries ago remains for me what Yeats called "the land of heart's desire" and what the old man speaking Frost's "To Earthward" longed to feel rough to all his length.

Some aestheticians believe that the lyric impulse begins with a crisis, a deep and long-lasting hurt, an experience that takes on dimensions of the traumatic: if anything, the girl—I have not seen her, except in dreams, for more than fifteen years—and the land, to which I return once or twice a year.

I have written, attempting to release some of the tension I

still feel, page after page of bad fiction. Now, writing this sentence, the girl and the land press heavily. I have the distinct impression that I can never live in the present unless I find some means of relieving the obsessions of the past. This smacks distastefully of therapy, but should the writer of memories manage to sound himself, should his sentences become the small stream that wears down the rock, he will have won.

The land and the girl consist of something that has nothing to do with plot, nothing to do with character, unless it is my own. The girl—I did not know this at the time—was not a person, but an object I invested with all the qualities that Gatsby credited to his Daisy. The land had more of a personality.

The word is "shine": her eyes, the dew of the grass, the rainbow mucus of earthworms, the bodies of fish, the surfaces of pondwater, the drops of a chicken's blood on its white feathers. The images I recall shine. I was never closer. It was as though these things shone from within, and for the first time.

(1972)

III

When, sixteen, I first left Long Island for the State University of New York College at Brockport I did not, could not know that if there is no going back, neither is it possible for me to forget the Island. Eliot asks: "What are the roots that clutch, what branches grow?"

The histories do not agree, but this is true enough to serve: in the seventeenth century Richard Smith, a farmer, was given by the Indians, in return for some guns and cattle and trinkets, as much land as he could encircle, riding bareback on a bull, in one day. Today Smith's bull stands, cast in bronze, glinting mapleshade from its horns, just off the Jericho Turnpike on the western edge of Smithtown, where Smith began and ended his ride. One summer, working for the town's highway department, I cut brush along Bread-and-Cheese Hollow Road where Smith stopped for lunch.

Nesconset, where I grew up, and St. James are two of the villages included in Smithtown Township. Over the harbor at St. James, a windmill, a Long Island landmark that made its way across the country on postcards, held the air with its great arms and cast its shadow on the water. The last hundred yards to the mill was a dirt road.

A door swung open on rusty hinges. I'd stand inside, letting my eyes adjust to the dark, until a well took shape in front of me. Then the stairs, about twenty sets bolted to the walls and curving upward at angles. All the way up cobwebs and spiderwebs, ropes and, somehow, branches swayed from a thatch of beams that blocked most of the light that made its way down from the door that opened to the mill's platform. The windmill was alive. Its steps and banisters creaked like bones. Small windows on the landings were its eyes. The wind whistled through broken wooden shingles.

Most of the ponds, once accessible only by paths through scrub-oak woods, have been bulldozed in. Children ride their bicycles on the sidewalks in front of homes built directly above what was once Shenandoah Pond in Nesconset. Also in Nesconset, Grove is gone, and most of Speck's, and most of Gibbs Pond.

In Smithtown, Miller's is almost gone, the pond behind

which a girl was murdered in 1953. She was seen leaving school with a tall, blond boy on her last afternoon. We were lined up in the halls of our schools while the teacher who had last seen the girl and her probable killer inspected us. But the case was never solved. I pictured the girl as having fallen asleep in the woods. I imagined a turtle, big as a house, rising from the mud of Miller's, crashing through the brush and slashing the girl's throat with its claws before lumbering back to its ooze. With red eyes it looked up through the dark water at its roof of lily pads.

My father had built his woodworking shop behind our house, but my three brothers and I were not as interested in his lathes and ripsaws or the stairs, windows, cabinets he built as we were in everything that went on at Wenzel's farm, adjacent to our property. Wenzel raised sheep, chickens, pheasants, rabbits. The earth in his pheasant pens was scattered with purple and gold feathers; the earth under the elm's limb from which he hung his slaughtered sheep and the earth under his chicken gallows was a deep red, almost black; the earth on Wenzel's farm smelled like manure and crushed apples and newly mown grass and the sweet, acrid body of a snake in your hands.

And of these things, Walt Whitman's Island wove the song of myself: the blue shadows of jays streaking across the shades of my bedroom at first light; a black ball of newly hatched catfish at Gibbs Pond; a lamb, a red and blue translucence, swaying from a branch, its nose dripping blood; a spider, with a scarlet gash on its body and big around as a butterfly, hanging from a single strand of web behind my father's shop; the three dogwoods on our front lawn covered with pink blossoms and as many bees; initials cut in the tar

70

roads, in the shingles of the mill, on the backs of box turtles, in the bark of trees; a blood-red cardinal that hurtled its body through the screen of a window beside my bed; a cow-bell, high up in an oak, clanking wildly in a hurricane wind; a cherry tree that dropped its fruit on our roof like rain; the gulls and V's of geese that passed overhead, washed in the yellow light; the long-fingered catalpas that lined our driveway.

IV

My stomach seems to empty and fill again as I drive over the humps and into the valleys of Gibbs Pond Road. It is dusk. The sky is shredded pink in the direction of Lake Ronkonkoma, which I plan to circle before driving home. I turn on the low beams, which make only vague impressions on the tar road. Just past the pond I cross Nichols Road and enter the shadows of the six huge elms that guard the corner.

I am driving very slowly. The car's windows are open and I can hear frogs serenading their log king, and small animals rustling the brush.

Three people are walking toward me on the other side of the road. I pass them under the elms. She is in the middle, and waves. Her father is with her, and another man. I do not think it strange that they would be walking along Gibbs Pond Road. It seems, rather, inevitable.

I do not wave, but pass them; then, regretting that I did not wave, I tap my horn ring, which emits a sound as of one more frog. I can hear everything. The hairs at the nape of my neck are bristling, and my ears seem to draw back and grow larger.

I am glad she saw the left side of my face, the side of my head where I comb my hair straight back, the side of myself I like best. I can still hear the three of them. They are laughing.

I look into my rearview mirror. She has not turned. She is wearing a white blouse and, if my eyes see correctly into the pools of darkness out of which the elms seem to be growing, she is holding hands with the other man.

A car is approaching from the direction of the lake. For a moment I concentrate on its headlights to make sure we will not collide, and once it has passed I slow down. My car is halfway up the rise of a small hump, and I slow down to a crawl.

I can see the other car's tail lights in my rearview mirror. The other car slows down and stops under the elms. I stop my car. I hear shouting, and then hear her scream. Looking back, I can see that the driver's door is open and that a dim light is on in the car. Its headlights are off.

I lift the automatic shift into reverse and, looking over my right shoulder at the whitish sand edge of the road, begin to back my car toward the shadows of the elms. I am aware of the noise of the woods above the hum of my car, and of an increasing hysteria of crickets.

. . . Watch it, someone yells, watch . . .

The rear wheels of my car whine in the mud and then slip backward into the pond. In a moment I am completely under water, holding my breath and trying to force the door open against the dark water. My strength seems useless. You fool, you fool, I say to myself. The door is jammed against the thick roots of lily pads and against elm branches.

V

My wife and I had spent our honeymoon in the Smokies and were driving north to Athens, Ohio, where we were to attend graduate school together.

The Tennessee and Kentucky roads we traveled were twisted and slow. More than once we'd pass over railroad tracks and a hundred feet further have to pass over the same tracks again. I thought of the spiral ascent to a tower in the mountains not far from Gatlinburg that overlooked several states.

Gatlinburg was like no city we had ever seen. Walking its garish main street one twilight, we had one of those moments when two people speak at the same time and say the same thing: "Long Island." But we'd had no reason to expect anything but a city that catered to tourists in general and honeymooners in particular. And we were pleased that we could walk through the candle shops and knickknack shops, that we could eat fine meals topped off with our first pecan pie, that we could play miniature golf a few feet from main street, or jump on trampolines, or drop paint on a piece of cardboard that spun on a wheel for thirty seconds. Our cabin at the motel was called Mountain Laurel.

We had met at Brockport four years before. I taught a year of high school English while she finished college. We were married in 1962, the date engraved inside our rings.

The road back from Gatlinburg was torturous. And my wife was afraid of the mountains. She'd talk to herself aloud and plan the perfect crime: we'd be shot, robbed, and buried, and our car hidden forever in one of the thousands of earth-colored barns behind rows of tall trees far off the roads. . . . When dark came on she sat quietly and watched the gas gauge.

Less than a year later, just before my Master's comprehensives, our son was born. We moved to Cortland, New York, where I taught at the college for two years, and then returned to Athens. Our daughter was born just before my Ph.D. examinations. We left for the good life once and for all in August of 1967. I'd waited as long as I could to hear about a job at Bennington (Roethke's old job, I fancied), but then decided to return to Brockport, not knowing, really, just what it was that drew me there. It was at Brockport that I'd suffered the loss of the girl and the land. I was not ready to return to the Island, which was now changing more rapidly than I could readjust its images. I had the distinct impression that, were I to return, I would drown. I knew some people in Brockport. I missed a row of magnificent poplars and the Erie Canal that cuts through the quiet town. I thought I would be able to write there where Mary Jane Holmes wrote her thirty-nine romances.

One man in Athens knew and understood. Richard Purdum, who directed my dissertation, is now dead.

When we sat in his office without talking, silence would hum. We would both look at the floor and wait for some deepest feeling to find its words. He would tell me of his insomnias, and of how he was progressing with the game he played: lying awake at night he'd organize the chaos of retinal imagery that danced against his eyelids. He'd gotten to the point where he could make the geometric shape he concentrated on appear, and in the desired color. The game, we knew, was important.

74

His poet was the Wallace Stevens of the deliberately believed-in fiction. He would read Stevens's *Collected Poems* through and then begin again. He'd been doing this for years. He was a small, thin, gentle man, and wonderfully sad. I could recognize his head-down shuffle across campus. When, in the halls or on the brick walks of the university, we approached each other, we would slow down, stop, and sometimes talk or sometimes just exchange helloes and move on. He might say: "Hey, I think I know what 'A Rabbit as King of the Ghosts' means," and tell me, finishing his explication with a series of "buts" that served to leave him where he began. Whenever I left him I was dizzy and he was entangled in speculations that would, no doubt, result in another sleepless night.

What carried him through his depressions and always would, I thought, was his sense of humor. When our eyes met, the expression on his face would seem to say that we were taking ourselves too seriously.

Two months after leaving graduate school I received a letter from him; six months later he was dead. He'd been on sabbatical, visiting relatives in Michigan. He'd bought a gun, and at break of spring, in a wooded area as wild as the old Island must have been and so remote his body was not found for weeks, had shot himself.

In a way I am guilty for not hearing the despair of the only letter I received from him. But now, looking at it as coldly as I am able, I also realize that his voice was the same as I'd known it over the years. In the letter, dated October 27, 1967, he wrote: "The weather has definitely changed this morning. It has been colder, there has been wind, I've been as blue, but the sound of the wind in today's trees is different, and I don't want to make out the words; so this letter will no doubt say nothing. . . ."

VI

And I am back again, this time walking along the south shore at Shinnecock Inlet. I am with Werner, my older brother. The tide is out. Skate eggs shine in the sand; sandfleas hum inside upside-down horseshoe crabs. I pick up a small piece of driftwood, soft as a sponge, so soft I can press my fingerprints into it, can see the whorls of my fingerprints against the grain of the wood.

We climb up on a jetty. Somehow, I've seen it before, from above, reaching out into the ocean like a spidercrab claw. Its rocks are fitted together like a jigsaw puzzle, like the continents pushed together on a map, becoming again the original land mass. We walk along the top, moving from one boulder to another. Shells and kelp and wine bottles dropped by fishermen are wedged between the rocks.

Straddling two rocks, I see something white in the shadows and crevices below me, maybe the belly of a fish, maybe a shell or a piece of paper or plastic or a lure snagged at high tide. But then I bend my neck and can't see it. But there are wide steps leading down among the rocks. I take off my shoes and descend, step after step, past walls of rock and sand, past the jawbone arches of whales scrawled with a nineteenth-century script I cannot read, past a wall of water, past a wall of mist I walk through like a ghost. My feet find the steps by themselves. My brother is calling:

. . . Bill, Bill, where are you going? What are you doing?

Then I am below his voice. The mist rolls away. I have reached bottom. I am in a cave floored with white sand, its ceiling supported by fluted columns of bone. I have not moved, but I have lost the stairs. I am alone in the cave, now wandering the floor of the Island, calling out, crying for someone to tell me where I am.

VII

The summer after my last year of high school, I developed a strain of encephalitis. At first, my parents thought I'd contracted polio, then were relieved that I hadn't, and then, when they became aware of what encephalitis could do, they became frightened again. In the beginning I couldn't move my legs, and I lost hope quickly. But my legs came back to life. Whether or not I sustained any brain damage, my brothers are fond of saying now, remains to be seen.

My recovery began, or at least my spirits revived, when I learned that the neurosurgeon who came around to stick pins into my legs was the doctor who worked with Roy Campanella after the Dodger catcher's automobile accident. Maybe the pros were still interested, I thought. Maybe they hadn't signed me at their tryouts that spring because I was only sixteen. I remember asking the doctor if I'd ever be able to play ball again. He said we'd see.

She visited me often, though I'm sure now that her affection for me had already grown thin and her visits to the hospital served to satisfy only her senses of martyrdom and duty. I was six feet four inches tall and down, at one point, to a hundred and twenty pounds. I was too listless to comb my hair and lay for hours listening to my records, especially the plaintive wail of a song by the Tune Weavers.

Before I left the Port Jefferson hospital I'd grown close to several of the nuns, one especially. Sister Mary Joseph, her neck rucked as a turtle's or the skin on your elbow, made an effort to combat my loss of weight with several orders of toast and jelly a day. Her old age and implacability helped me keep my own problems in perspective. It is in their eyes that old people seem to hold the difficult knowledge absorbed during their long lives. Her irises were gray and bottomless as an animal's. They told me not to be afraid, and I wasn't. I was a Lutheran, but felt that I shared her God.

When I drive along the Hudson River, or on the Skyway into Buffalo, or along the Jericho through Smithtown Branch where great locusts shade the traffic, I think of how wild and beautiful the Island must have been. Is it inhuman to say there is no such thing as an improvement of nature? Just as cold is simply the absence of heat and there is, so far as we know, no such thing as absolute cold, we ought to measure our architecture, our rearrangement of the landscape, in terms of how little it offends nature, which is right, perfect, unfathomable, rhythm within rhythm. Offend we do and must when we lay down even a flagstone walk or build a cabin by the side of a lake. Were we all to disappear, it would take only a generation for lily of the valley and wild roses to break through the pavement of Times Square. Our bridges would fall into the rivers and be buried like the skeletons of beasts. Smith's bull, if there is spirit in metal, would stamp its hoofs as the old Island again broke into being.

Deep in the woods behind our house a foundation was sinking, ferns were growing up through the two-by-fours and

78

shingles spread about, and gnarled apple trees were merging with the underbrush; and when I left the hospital that summer and walked through the woods again I thought on these things. I fancied myself as powerful as Gulliver among the little people, and force-fed every human being on earth a capsule of poison. To allow the world to live, I was ready to die, if only everyone else would die at the same time. I am still not sure that our will to survive and prevail is not a negative courage.

VIII

The movie house in which I am sitting is cavernous. Bats hang from its ceiling like black gourds. The air is cool and smells slightly of lilac and fern.

The screen is a square of white in the dark. A shaft of white light appears over my head and then takes color. The screen's white curtains part. She is walking on the sidewalk in front of her father's barbershop. Music begins, a sad ballad by The Platters. She walks across the steet and waits at the curb. The music stops.

She is wearing her graduation robe. The robe's sleeves fill out in a wind that also blows her hair back from her forehead. The only sound is the sound of leaves rustling from the maples behind her. The film stands still for a long time as she waits by the curb. The film jumps and her sleeves again fill with wind. She waves. I pretend she is not waving to me. A hearse (for this, I think, is a melodrama without end) stops in front of her and blocks her from my sight. As it pulls away I can just make out her profile past the flowers and through the

79

glare of the hearse's back window. I don't know if she is in the hearse or is still standing by the curb.

The camera shifts across the street to the window of her father's shop. I do not see myself, but see a reflection of myself in the glass. I can see only my back. My hands are in my pockets. The camera moves left and I see myself, from the back, standing with my hands in my pockets. I turn around and see myself sitting in the dark. We are both crying.

IX

I want to capture, in part, the essential stillness of the Island, its nonhuman being, someone's mind moving upon its silence. It is difficult for me to know where I fit in, or which of my selves is involved. I lived what might be called an archetypal American boyhood. My Island, at first Huckleberry Finn's territory, is now, certainly, Willy Loman's territory, land of the big sale and the big kill. Oaks over the Smithtown Bypass have hollows in their trunks where the gunshots of a gangland rub-out still reverberate. All over the Island softballs hit foul drop through trees around the lighted diamonds behind which knives flash and old men are mugged.

It is June, 1971. The Southerner would know, and the New Englander, what I, returning to Long Island to rest and write, feel. In Suffolk the land has been touched more rapidly and violently than anywhere else in the country except, perhaps, for a few counties in California. It would take generations to see these changes in other parts of the country. I have no choice but to let go of the land as it was. I want to package that part of my life here, the love-hate relationship I now have with it, wrap it up, leave it. It may be my desire for the hard voice, the poem with an edge of rage, that causes me to need to burn memorial bridges to the Island. But I have already walked the edges of our property here and chosen four small trees—an oak, maple, dogwood, spruce— to plant in Brockport, and in so doing have already weakened the possibility of severing roots.

Men do not understand that this is a land that brings in topsoil by truck rather than time. Many, like Wenzel, grow strange. I cut back some weeds along his fence this morning. He watched me work and then walked over. Wenzel had lived here ten years before we moved here. He once had thirty acres of woods, thousands of chickens and pheasants, dozens of sheep, but ended up as a salesman in J. C. Penney's. He had whistled as he worked his farm, the hair on his shoulders glistening. He would rub manure on his chest and tell my brothers and me that the earth cured everything from warts to Weltschmerz. Wenzel, who was the happiest, most self-sufficient man I had ever known, who years ago had made an egg run to New York City every Friday night, was now afraid of the traffic, the new neighbors, the spotlights in the sky announcing new shopping centers. And he is now a foxhole convert.

Wenzel has gotten old and, as an old German saying goes, *"Wenn Leute alt werden, werden sie wunderlich"* (when people grow old, they get odd). This morning Wenzel lectured me on the impending return of Christ. He told me that I had nothing unless I had Christ. He shouted hallelujahs so loud that my mother's cat ran off. Wenzel, once the disciple of the earth and cynical of all prophets, had gotten himself some religion in a hurry. He spends his time rocking in his back yard and laughing out loud: they are all fools rushing by in the streets out there past his hedges. Heaven is Wenzel's personal pastoral. Heaven shall restore the things that once were.

And he is the rule rather than the exception. It takes the fingers of both hands to count the old neighbors who walk their yards talking very loudly to themselves. At Kings Park Hospital the Old Professor, as we used to call him, sweeps a section of lawn under the trees with an imaginary broom and guides down a flying saucer. Here in Nesconset, spiritual spaceships land every day. But not birds.

For picture Wenzel, lovable old madman, down in his basement workshop, among old candlers and egg washers. Chuckling to himself, he hinges together an elaborate construction of boards, shows his invention to his wife. And when he hears jays in his pines or crows at the top of his oaks, he rushes outside and sets up a racket and clatter and consternation with his boards. Picture this daughterless Lear, this child of this emerald Island, his wordless heart raging faster and louder than his boards.

X

A Model A rusted on the shore of Gibbs Pond. One door was locked shut and one swung on one busted hinge. We fished from its hood. It spread a circle of rust into the pond. We did not think of the rust as poison, but thought it drew the fish toward our bobbers. . . . The history of one small shop along the Jericho: Guarini's Pet Shop became Helen's Drapes became Midas Muffler became Greg's Lawn Mower

Service became Uncle's Florist became Garage Door Alarms became Ed's Automotive. . . . . The Japanese beetle, its back a myriad of metallic sheens, when it feasts on a grape leaf seems not to destroy but to uncover the leaf's hidden form and beauty, Michelangelo chipping away excess stone. The beetle leaves behind the leaf's white tracery of veins, or, to change the image, its skeleton. Our grape arbor after one onslaught of beetles fifteen years ago was white, unearthly, ghostly. From a distance it seemed the whorl of a great spider. . . . In "The Open Boat" one of Crane's characters says that gulls seem to have been carved with a jackknife. The clumsy artisan, of course, is the god of fate, or chance, or irony, who drowns the strongest crewman. The gulls that passed over Nesconset were sleek, silent; they glided over our property without a single wingbeat. They flew lower than the V's of geese or the circling hawks, but higher than the starlings or Werner's pigeons. The gulls, every day of the year, headed to the Sound on a straight line. They seemed white as bone, clean as icicles. When I saw them up close at the Sound or at St. James Harbor they were jagged and dirty and raucous. I remember thinking that these had to be different gulls, these scavengers. These could not be the same gulls that washed themselves in the light over Nesconset. . . . He was the most popular and promising of us all, began to drink heavily and became an alcoholic by twenty. He was involved in a freak accident: one night he ran his sports car into a highway department truck that had rolled down from its parking place and waited for him on the Bypass. Scarred and crippled, he won a large settlement from the Town of Smithtown, threw away thousands in two months over one bar. Became an addict. Is now institutionalized. . . . Terlik, another neighbor, cooked a half bushel of blueclaws at a time. The brilliant colors: the crabs (their blue luster, their shades of blue enamel), sprigs of parsley added, then a cup of salt and sliced lemons. Tonged out of the boiling water, the crabs were bright orange. . . . Remembered because of violence: Wenzel's terrier up on its hind legs fighting a rat almost as big as itself; his chicken gallows, the cutting of throats, white chickens running headless, splashing blood on themselves; a black cat with a Baltimore oriole in its jaws; bludgeoning the sandsharks drawn up from the deep waters past Crane's Neck in the Sound. . . . Mrs. Patac's memories of Lake Avenue, once a dirt path under oaks, neighbors visiting one another on Sundays in horse-drawn carts, gifts of cakes, baskets of squash and wildflowers plucked along the way. . . . I dream I am barefoot, walking the edges of Gibbs Pond. I sink to my knees in mud. Trees grow out of the water, their roots raised—cypress, a thousand years old, dark and alien to the Island. It is evening. The pond becomes a swamp. But I still wade among the roots of the trees. I'm trying to catch tropical fish, swordtails and tetras that glow orange and green and dull yellow in the dark water. . . . When I turned over a rock in the woods, I'd lean close and my skull's shadow would seem to fill, even blossom with small things: slugs and worms, glazed in mucus, would contract like bits of muscle; beetles, spiders, ants balancing blue eggs ran for the security of the leaves; fire-red centipedes, thin tongues of flame, licked in and out of tunnels. . . . I was clamming in the harbor's soft swells. It was a beautiful evening. Something touched the back of my knee. It felt like a hand of feathers. It was a dead gull. In a rat's nest, in a sprinkling of bones, under one corner of the garage, I found a robin, eyeless as the gull but otherwise still whole. . . . I once dreamed that I tangled in the branches of the great tree at the center of the lake and drowned, but breathed water like a fish, and sang in its blue branches like a bird. . . . 1796: Long Island's first lighthouse erected at Montauk Point; described by Gabriel Furman (1874) as "a very massive and durable tower of stone"; but September 21, 1815: gale winds shatter its lantern: the lighthouse stands dark as a tree over the jagged rocks: ships search for its light over the whitecaps, search for the lantern, search for its star above the duned glacier of the sea: too long ago not to remember: before the glacier receded from the Island: before it left a fish with two flukes, melted to lakes: Panamoka, bottomless Ronkonkoma: before it left the Island under the stars, under the hot sun to leaf to beauty: white and black oak, hickory, dogwood, locust, fragrant cedar: before the shorebirds: too long ago not to remember: before the changeless crab that now drags its ridged dagger through the sands and mud flats: before the bluefish, bass, buffalo whose hoofs still thunder in shells: in the beginning: before the Indians, before the colonists, before Smith, before Washington rode through Smithtown Branch and stopped at the Widow Blydenburgh's and wrote in his diary: "The fields and woods are died red with berries": too long ago not to remember: before the farmers of the salt meadows of marsh grass: before the Southampton and Sag Harbor whalers: before even the dream of it: before the glacier descended, heaved, split, receded: before the lighthouse at Montauk lost its lantern to gale winds, waves swept the edges of an island, wind sang in the dark branches of a shore. . . . William Bradford (1630): "And though it was very dark and rained sore, yet in the end they got under the lee of a small island and remained there all that night in safety. . . ." Seon Manley (1966): "On Long Island, time, tide, and the wind have moved with frightening splendor. Add to the picture the increase of tropical storms and one can grasp some shadow of our future. Each century is marked by a rise of two more feet of ocean level." Ralph Henry Gabriel (1921): "Long Island lies offshore like a giant tree, uprooted and fallen in the water, its trunk and branches half submerged."

XI

We are lying down somewhere in the woods, covered only by a thin blanket of leaves. It is nearly dark. I am worried that she will awaken and not want to spend the night here with me. I touch her hair. I do not know whether I am talking to her or whether the words I hear are only in my mind. I do not understand all of the words, but I know this is the first time, perhaps because she is asleep, that I have been able to use words this way, words I did not even know I knew. But I also know I am not the self, here at this time, that I should be. I am older, or I have somehow learned the words that tell what I feel, or the words are in the leaves that cover us.

. . . You have, though we are this young, been what I have been and needed with the knowledge that goes before us, that built this Island from its force, that will go on after us.

There is a slight wind high in the leaves of the oaks above us.

. . . I want you to know that what we have is forever inviolate; that in the beginning the stars knew this moment, and the dark trees; that we, who have never touched, were born in the roots of these dark trees. There is a poem I almost remember in whose shade there is a pool of clear water we have both, unknowingly, lain down beside.

My eyes have adjusted to the dark. The wind moves branches now.

. . . I want to tell you. There are forgotten meanings in the Noh, in the arrangements of tea leaves; there are lines in the psalms of fathoms; there are words in the blue irises of shadows; there is something we cannot ruin. I mean the sun is a flower rooted in darkness, whose roots are darkness.

It is too cold for us here, but the wind increases and more and more leaves fall to cover us and keep us warm. My hands rake leaves over her. The wind seems high above us, seems to hack stars from their nests in the trees.

. . . Listen. In the beginning there were trees in far forests that bent to the arrows of wind like bows, that were felled and curved to the bows of ships of our fathers' fathers, who said their sons' sons and daughters shall lie here under the trees on just such a windship of night, and one shall say to another, as I am saying now, I think I have always known that I have said what I can say and can say no more, until, whether or not we meet again in the far countries, I shall again say as I now shake words like leaves out of the branches of my tongue, you have not forgotten, could not forget.

The words stop. Now oak leaves cover me completely. I would be able to sleep if I knew for certain she still slept beside me under the leaves. I hear the trees above me, like the branches of my foolish heart, begin to rage. But never, before this moment, have I heard as clearly the inescapable sirens of the trees. She is not beside me. She never was.

XII

In 1643 local Indian tribes were preoccupied with defending themselves against Mohawk marauders from the west. One William Kreft of the West India Company, who claimed he had purchased Long Island from the Indians, chose this time to perpetrate atrocities against Island tribes. David De Vries, the first owner of Staten Island, knew Kreft. These paragraphs, which describe events that took place on the night of February 25, 1643, are from De Vries's diary:

"The Wannekens, as they call the Dutch, had done it. . . . When it was day the soldiers returned to the fort, having massacred or murdered eighty Indians, and considering they had done a deed of Roman valor, in murdering so many in their sleep, where infants were torn from their mothers' breasts, and hacked to pieces in the presence of the parents, and the pieces thrown into the water, and other sucklings, being bound to small boards, were cut, stuck, and pierced, and miserably massacred in a manner to move a heart of stone. . . .

"Some came to our people in the country with their entrails in their arms, and others had such horrible cuts and gashes, that worse than they could never happen. And these poor simple people, as also many of our own people, did not know any better than they had been attacked by a party of other Indians. . . . After this exploit, the soldiers were rewarded for their services, and Director Kreft thanked them by taking them by the hand and congratulating them."

As the frontier moved west and as the white man consolidated his gains on the Island and as weaponry grew more sophisticated, corpse was piled on corpse. To be sure, he had his reasons, motives. His mind defended him against his heart. His mirror images stared back at him self-righteously. Those from whom he had something to gain were better off dead.

Washington Irving describes Sleepy Hollow: "A drowsy, dreamy influence seems to hang over the land, and to pervade the very atmosphere." Today, on the Island, people have triple-locked their doors, and for good reason. Who knows what madmen prowl the streets? Half-wit cowboys pound their fists on the bars, shout that "if guns are outlawed only outlaws will have guns," and drink until their beer joints close. The insane are let out on probation from the over-crowded hospitals that dot the Island. Kids gun their rods and blast out streetlamps with shotguns and deer rifles. Deranged veterans haunt the dark carrying bayonets in their back pockets.

Using a rifle as a cane, I am walking Lake Avenue to St. James. I remember Hawthorne's darkest sentence: "The road grew wilder and drearier and more faintly traced, and vanished at length, leaving him in the heart of the dark wilderness, still rushing onward with the instinct that guides mortal man to evil." I begin to feel my own power. I am capable of any crime. A patrol car slows down as it passes, and I shout at it, dare it to stop. I have not walked in the dark for years and experience, now, an intense satisfaction in the knowledge that the people who pass me in their cars are afraid of me, a furtive figure in a dark jacket. In the black and fragrant shade of the dogwoods that line the road, time and space expand to timelessness, morality to amorality, until a thought that has always been on my mind, the thought that it would be of no true universal consequence were I to enter a home and kill its inhabitants as they sleep, that this act would in no way matter, becomes a truism, becomes an emotional and intellectual fact. But not for long. And I am not afraid of them. They have not harmed me or threatened my sense of myself, and they have nothing I want.

XIII

That tree, the glory of our back yard, gave way at last to Hurricane Nancy who arrived at mid-century and, bitch that she was, surprised us with how much she could take away.

That tree was a wild cherry—I smile at my own obsession with it—but it was the "great-rooted blossomer" of a chestnut and "spreading laurel" of Yeats's poems: it was, as Padraic Colum describes Yggdrasill, the evergreen ash rooted in Icelandic mythology, a "tree that spread its branches through all the worlds," through all the worlds of time.

When the cherry fell it did not split, but descended intact, uprooting the earth, baring a half acre of grass to the storm. We worked for several days, in Nancy's dying tailwinds, chopping the tree up and carting it away. Those nights the tree hovered its ghost, continued its reawakening to another April, refused to fall, refused to break, still supported its nests of songbirds, still swung the bulb of a pair of orioles that returned each year to the Island, still shook with dark red fruit, still dripped prisms of rain from its leaves.

Years later, when I thought only the tree's burnt stump remained, I went down into our cellar to look for something, kneeled on the cement, and noticed that the cherry's roots had broken through the foundation of the house. Perhaps the roots strengthened the house, as they sometimes strengthen the walls of a cistern; perhaps the tree eventually would have brought our house down.

We still have photographs of various family arrangements under the tree. Our faces are shadows. And the moment the cherry fell our house grew lighter, as though candles had been lit in each room. But the tree shaded our house in burning summer.

I balance memories: the tree drew flocks of starlings down from the sky like dark leaves and, winter nights, threw a terrible skeletal silhouette against the house; but its branches held the full summer and shook brilliant after rain, and its loss led me to need words. Since it fell I have tried to live as though I would have it fall again.

XIV

The seats in this small plane are numbered from one to thirty. Number thirty is in the left front and Billy, my son, who is seven now and with me, holds to edges of seats until he gets to seat thirty, where I'm sitting, but it's too high for him there, the plane is swaying and lurching like a bus, and there are gaps in the floor and the floor is shifting as the metal floor between railroad cars seems to shift, and we're high above the earth, so he makes his way across the aisle to seat seven.

. . . What can we do? he asks.

. . . It's all right, I shout above the racket of the plane's engine, we'll make it.

I tell him that he couldn't fit through one of those holes

in the floor if he wanted to. He laughs happily, hysterically.

Our pilotless plane is hurtling downward now, and now, somehow, I am lying down on my stomach, controlling the plane with my weight as though it were a bobsled. We must land. We must land somewhere. I can make out the Sound below, then St. James Harbor, then Lake Avenue where it crosses the Jericho.

We are down now, scraping pavement crazily in this plane without wheels, whipping along, past Brown's Road and the hardware store, past the telephone company warehouse. We veer onto Gibbs Pond Road where it forks away from Lake, the fire department whizzes past us on our left, then the school, and our luck is still holding out because even one car would do us in. We are still going fast, our wings are just making it between telephone poles on both sides of the road. Billy is screaming somewhere behind me. We're past Zauzin's farm now, half flying and half scraping toward the Bypass intersection swarming with cars and will never, I know, stop in time, and suddenly night has fallen, we're whipping over the slight hump of blacktop past Zauzin's, and I decide quickly to lift and shift my weight right, and do, and the plane lifts slightly, we just make it over Terlik's hedge, between his hedge and the telephone wires scrawled against the darkness, we just make it onto his field, the only open area around. We settle down, still moving fast, but slowing now, grass underneath us now like lily pads under a rowboat, and I tell Billy to keep his head down and his hands inside and I tell him something about biting down on his sleeve, and I am wondering whether we will stop before we crack into the grape arbors or the barn beyond the open field when I realize we have stopped. We've stopped. I roll out of the plane onto the grass. Billy is with me. We both yell that we've made it, we've made it. We roll in the grass. We have never, I know, been so happy. The grass is wet with the night's dew and thick as clover and a dark, dark green, and smells so sweet.

XV

Someone is reaching out his arms toward Long Island Sound and is weeping. I approach his silhouette across a dark lawn. I am only vaguely interested in his problem, whatever it is; in fact, I am intensely happy about my own life at this moment as I approach this poor fellow holding his arms out toward the waters I used to crab and clam. I have no idea what is wrong with him or why he is carrying on this way. Is he an actor in the heat of a soliloquy? Is he about to commit suicide?

He steps into the water. At that moment there is a blare of lights in the trees past an acre of lawn behind him. I can see outlined there what must be his house, huge and incoherent, lit up like a birthday cake. He must be very rich to have a house like that, I think.

I walk over to where he is standing in the water. He is still holding his arms out to the Sound's blank face.

I tap him on the shoulder. He turns to me. He is not surprised to see me there, but I am surprised to see how much he resembles me. Still, I am relieved that I am not him. I know who he is. He is Joe McCloy. I would know Joe even though I have seen him only three times before. Even though I know that he lost Karen as I did, I wonder if she is in his house. For a moment I think I can make her out coming across the lawn to where Joe and I are standing ankle-deep in the water. No, she isn't there. It is only a deer that turns around and moves away from us again.

. . . Why the hell are you continuing to cry this way? I ask him. What are you doing?

. . . I am eating my bitter heart, he answers. Tears are streaming down his cheeks in the moonlight in this incessant foolish lamentation of a soap opera I seem doomed to live through to some whimper of a conclusion. He says: I am eating my bitter heart out. His face is a farcical caricature of the weeping Christ. He says: I am eating my own bitter heart out, but I like it because it is bitter, and because it is my heart.

XVI

There's a poem by Gary Snyder called "Hay for the Horses" in which an old man says he'll be damned if he didn't go ahead and spend fifty years of his life bucking hay. But Snyder, I think, likes this fellow. And the old man is not angry, really, or discontented. He's wistful, and he's amazed that life could have gone by so quickly. The poem is about the old man's love for his life as he has lived it. He is just beginning to understand his commitment to a quotidian of haydust and grasshoppers and shingle-cracks of barnlight. He says:

> I first bucked hay when I was seventeen.
> I thought, that day I started,

I sure would hate to do this all my life.
And damnit, that's just what
I've gone and done.

But it has been a good life for him, and he knows it. The life *is* the work, and he has chosen perfectly. He knows that he could have done differently, but never knew where he was likely to go better.

There's a character in one of the sketches of *Winesburg, Ohio* so upset with what he in his own life has come to be that "Every time he raised his eyes and saw the beauty of the country in the failing light he wanted to do something he had never done before, shout or scream or hit his wife with his fists or something equally unexpected and terrifying." This is a deep sentence, and one psychologically true. Sherwood Anderson went inside of himself for it.

Ray Pearson is the character's name. He feels that his own years have been mean, that his marriage has been only a burden, his thin-legged children only millstones. Oh, what might have been, say so many of Anderson's characters. They are caught up in feelings of yearning so vague and obscure that we complement their pain with our own. The difference between Snyder's old man and Ray Pearson is that Pearson never feels complete. He is angry and frustrated. He feels that he had it inside himself to become so much more. He feels that he has wasted his life.

I take it that this has nothing to do with Truth. A man, says Anderson, becomes a grotesque when he fastens upon and commits himself to the reality of one of his fictions. Of the book's dozens of characters, Doctor Reefy seems the most balanced and speaks best for his creator. We think of Anderson when the good Doctor writes his momentary truths and systems on bits of paper, rolls the papers into little balls, and, when he has too many of them, throws them in the face of a "blithering old sentimentalist." Yes, it may be that the man who believes in anything at all is a sentimentalist. But it may be, as Wallace Stevens says in his magnificent "The World as Meditation," that the planet sometimes encourages. It may be that some men seem bent on establishing an adversary relationship with the world that costs so much more in joy and love than is necessary. And the sort of character who moves past even Doctor Reefy's balanced cynicism to a life blessed by being at ease with its own imperfections is nowhere to be found in *Winesburg*. We are left to think of Anderson, the man himself, writing, writing, writing all those memories and dreams in all those lonely rooms in all those slums.

XVII

Carbone's place was across Gibbs Pond Road and about a hundred yards past our house. The Wenzels had a house, the Zauzins had a house, we had a house, but Carbone's place was just a tarpaper shack, square and dirty, its flat roof sagging and streaked by residues of leaves and pine needles. This was, I think, 1950, but I can see Carbone's place still, shadowy and squatting back off the road among oaks and pines like a great toad. And I've only now realized what was so different about Carbone's yard: he didn't have one. We and the Wenzels and the Zauzins had a lawn and hedges and even rows of trees. Carbone's yard was scrub oak, scrub pine, thistles, goldenrod and ragweed and piles of sand left over from some old cement project. Along one side of his property garbage rattled and blew down a slight ravine, a rat and snake heaven.

I would see him only every few weeks or so. Winter or summer, he'd be wearing an overcoat that reached to his ankles and a floppy hat that reached to his ears. He'd be pulling a rusty child's wagon or pushing a rusty wheelbarrow filled with empty bottles that had lost their labels. Where he was going or what he was doing with all those bottles or where he got them I don't remember, if I ever knew. I do know that I never heard him say a single word, never heard him shout or laugh or even mutter.

Carbone was only a moment's curiosity for us when, on the way to swimming or to a ball game or to a hill on Southern Boulevard for some sledding, we passed him. Something seemed to be wrong with his eyes, as though there were too much white in them and too little iris. But there were two meetings with him that I do remember.

The first time, I was selling seeds. I must have been in about the fourth grade. Something possessed me to try Carbone. The side door to his shack was half open. I knocked on its tarpaper shingles and saw at the same time some movement inside. I stepped inside and saw Carbone sitting at a table, facing me, his hat on, fumbling at an egg, trying to peel it. I backed away. I didn't know if he had seen me.

And then there was the autumn day I was walking back from school along the side of the road that brought me directly past Carbone's shanty and I saw him stretched out flat on his back, almost hidden by patches of thistles and weeds. I stepped across his property only halfway to where he lay, only close enough to see his eyes staring straight up through the fall trees that were blowing leaves down around him. I think he was breathing, and I remember thinking that old men were queer fellows and perhaps Carbone had just fallen asleep outside and did not have a hammock. But something frightened me. I ran home and told my mother. Then I forgot about Carbone. It was months later before I realized I didn't see him around any more, that that afternoon I saw him staring his white eyes toward the autumn skies was the last time I'd seen him.

Maybe ten years later some of his relatives knocked his shack down and built a new house, one with a yard, on the property. The garbage ravine is filled in now, and the name on a new mailbox says *Carbone* in gold letters, and some of the little kids who play there now must be grandchildren, or great-grandchildren of the man I didn't know.

XVIII

There was a stretch of shore at Short Beach that was all stones, millions of stones, and not just a single layer, but deep. The largest stones were as big as maybe your hand. You could walk along the water's edge, trusting the summer's callouses on your feet or the smoothness of most of the stones, and could let your mind wander over the kingdom of stones at your feet, until a different color or striation or glitter of mica or something stopped your eye and you bent down and reached into the cold clear water for that particular stone.

This is where we were, the four of us, I'm sure. But I was not really part of what was happening. I was watching. I couldn't see myself, but I was watching, standing at the edge of the water, looking at the other three men, one to the left side on a dune of stones, two kneeling in the stones. The one on the left wore a serape, and was back-lit, the sun falling behind him and outlining his profile in red-gold. His arms were raised; he was facing the other two, and his shadow fell across to them. But it was somehow a white shadow, gray-white, only slightly darker than the day. He stood there, I thought, like the statue of Jesus overlooking Rio de Janeiro. And he was silent, holding up his arms, his serape falling gracefully around him. No, it was a gown, it was as long as a gown, and its bottom folds grew to marble. He was that statue, but he was not. It was a serape, and he was a man I knew. I knew his gossamer hair, his glasses. I knew how his voice would sound were he to talk or laugh. But he was silent, and still. But the two men kneeling in the sand were moving and talking. And I knew them too, and could name them. And they knew one another, I knew, and had for a long time. There was a pile of stones between them, stones through which the light shone, stones that glowed. And the one man—I felt that I didn't like him, didn't understand him—was passing the stones to the man I loved, was asking him to name them. And then I knew I was right for what I felt about them. And behind them the dying sun shone through the man in the serape onto the two men kneeling in the stones. And the man I didn't like picked up one stone. And that stone was beautiful to me. It was as beautiful as the bloom of an iris, and was somehow translucent, and I wanted to hold it, and my eyes filled with tears. The man I didn't like handed that stone to the man I loved and asked, impatiently, "What should we call this one, what should we call this one, what should we call this one, what should we call this one?" And the man I loved weighed the stone tenderly in his hands and held it close to his eyes and then at arms' length and said, "We will call this blue. We will call this steep blue." His voice tightened my throat. He spoke again. He said, "We will call this stone a steep, steep blue."

XIX

From *Webster's Geographical Dictionary* (1949): Island, SE of New York and S of Connecticut, lying bet. Long Island Sound on N and Atlantic Ocean on S; 118½ m. long, 23 m. at greatest width; 1401 sq. m. (including water, 1723 sq. m.); pop. 4,600,022; comprises Suffolk, Nassau, Queens, and Kings cos. of New York state; borough of Brooklyn (Kings co.) at its SW extremity. At W end separated from the Bronx and Manhattan by East river and from Staten I. by the Narrows. Has 280 m. of coast line indented by numerous inlets and bays, esp. Peconic and Gardiners Bays at E end and Great South and Jamaica Bays on S shore. Hilly along N shore; has many fine beaches along the S (Rockaway, Jones, Fire Island, Coney Island). At its E end is Montauk Point with several large islands in adjacent waters (Shelter, Gardiners, Plum, etc.). Has grown to be great residential district for New York City. . . . Included in grant to Plymouth Co. by James I, 1620; conveyed to William Alexander, Earl of Stirling, 1635; became part of British colony of New York by treaty, 1674; earliest settlement by Dutch 1623, and by English, ab. 1640; scene of battle of Long Island (at Brooklyn Heights) in Revolutionary War, Aug. 27, 1776, in which Lord Howe defeated Americans under Washington, who, however, successfully withdrew his forces across the river.

XX

I am walking down steps again. This time the steps are narrow blocks of hewn stone, and curve as though I am walking down the steeple of a great cathedral embedded in the earth. The fingers of my right hand trace the line of my descent on the wet stones of the wall, my feet move easily into the depressions of the stone steps. I am holding a candle in my left hand, its flame gusting toward me and then away. I am descending the stairs as fast as the candle will allow me. But it goes out anyway. I stop. But the stone steps and the stone walls are not as black as the black air, and I can still move down the stairs. I feel curiously at ease, as though some part of me knows where I am going and is unafraid. I feel it is right that I am walking down these stairs. I descend the stairs for a long, long time, thinking of nothing that could serve to fill the dark.

Now one of the wallstones seems to glow with blue lines, but no image appears. Now I can make out the profile of a snout, coyote or wolf, glowing with a dull pearl light from another wallstone. Now the flank of a horse glowing a beautiful rose-red from the stone ceiling. And now I am entering a chamber so overwhelming that I have to close my eyes to its walls and ceiling. For this is the chamber of reverence. Eyes and horns adorn the stones, buffalo and bear and pheasant, each animal standing out from the stones in the color of blood or pearl or pale sunlight or grass. I have so much to learn here. Buffalo and bear and pheasant, otter and owl, boar and fox and wolf and horse. When I see them it is as though I hear their names for the first time. And now I know. I know that at a moment like this I must hold my breath. I must allow the animals to find me in the air of the dark chamber. If I clear my mind, if I believe for once in my life in silence, if I disavow declaration . . .

I sit down on grass under the sky of this cave back where the land began. There is plenty of time. I will wait here for everything and for nothing. I will, at last, be still.

XXI

One morning a long time ago my mother came running into the house as though Indians were after her. She finally gasped out that she'd been picking strawberries in the patch way in back of our property against the woods when she stepped right into the coil of a snake. If she really did step into a circle of snake, it was probably just a harmless garter sunning itself or taking advantage of the worked loam and strawberry shade.

But another time, while outside hanging laundry to dry, my mother screamed and did have something to scream about. She said that a cat had run out of the woods straight at her and attacked her. We could see that her left calf had been punctured by at least four teeth.

Cats were a problem for us back then. The Suffolk woods were home to the offspring of domestic cats that had littered in the wild. The generations flourished there, and grew wild again. We could hear the cats' screams as they fought. One of my most vivid memories is the night sound of teeth against bone outside my bedroom window, not a grinding sound but almost a cluck, a horrible liquid tear as though of knuckles and joints popping apart, or the sound of your jaw if you momentarily dislocate it. One morning I found two dead toms under a rhododendron. Both were torn apart, shreds of fur, ripped eyes and nostrils.

We had three rifles in the family, three 22's. I had a single shot, my father and older brother Werner had clip models. We killed dozens of cats over the years. Cats would scream outside at night and we would go out in slippers, shine a flashlight into the dark, and fire bullets between their slashes of yellow and green eyes.

There was another summer morning I can still see clearly. My brother and I had fired at a cat during the night. For some reason, we'd both fired birdshot; we were sure we'd hit that cat, that some pellets had found it in the dark, but were pretty sure we hadn't killed it. It took 22-longs to kill cats. When we walked outside that morning we heard snarling at the edge of our property and approached what was apparently the cat we'd shot. It raged at us, rocked on three legs, one eye flashing in the morning shine, one closed and weeping blood. It was the biggest cat we had ever seen, a red, but its coat almost one solid rust, not quite like other reds we'd seen. It crossed my mind that this was a real wildcat.

We ran inside for our guns, ran back to the cat, knelt down on one knee about twenty feet away from it and fired, almost together. The cat seemed to rear up and throw itself back over its own shoulder. It didn't drop. It took to the woods, dragging one useless leg. We followed, certain it would die. I knew that my bullet had hit it full in the chest.

We waded through lily of the valley, its millions of small white bells, that bordered that' edge of our property. We walked through ferns that blanketed the wood's floor under the oaks, and followed the snarling cat. We were both afraid of this cat but never considered not following it and making sure it was dead. I already felt, also, sick at heart, felt that this cat was more than the other cats, more important, that I was in another dimension, another world, desecrating that world, that this was somehow personal, that this cat knew me, that something outside ourselves was bearing witness to this whole episode to which I was somehow committed. These were the woods of the old Island; this was center Island, the awful power of its perfumes.

About a hundred yards deep in the woods we caught up to the cat. I remember ducking under some brush into a small clearing, the cat again only about twenty feet away, at the base of a tree, its back arched, its rust fur matted with blood. Werner and I knelt there and fired. My hands managed to fumble four or five bullets into the chamber of my rifle. I fired directly into the cat's face and could see the bullets strike, could see round spots of blood appear as the bullets entered its twisted face. Werner must have fired the eight shots of his clip. But the cat wouldn't fall, wouldn't fall, but didn't attack us as I was afraid it would, until it finally did fall, its front paws still jerking, still clutching for something it could tear apart. It did fall, did stop snarling. I dropped my rifle, sat down, breathed deep, tried to get hold of myself. It was only another cat, I told myself.

XXII

I have not had a memorable dream for months. But last night I dreamed and woke up and remembered, then fell back asleep and dreamed again and woke up and remembered again, then fell asleep and dreamed a third dream. I don't know why, unless: in three weeks, after ten months here in Germany, we'll be flying back to America. And when we fly back to America we will be flying back to Long Island for ten days before we drive back to Brockport.

First, I am far away from home. I am to give a poetry reading at a college. Yes, I am in California, where she still lives. No, I am at William Smith in Geneva walking across rolling lawns shaded by groves of great elms under which there are marble benches and chairs. She is somewhere, I know. I remember phoning her when I arrived, picturing her as we spoke on the phone: she is older, has lines on her forehead and around her mouth, and she is sad, but smiles as we talk. But I am walking the lawns now looking for her. Didn't we make an appointment? And where was it to be? Just what did we say on the phone? I am sweating and my feet are beginning to hurt. I have slung my suit jacket over my shoulder and rolled up the sleeves of my white shirt. I am becoming frustrated. I am lost in a grove of trees and will never find her, at least not here. Anger and humiliation. I shout something obscene. I sit down in a marble chair. It is as though I am in a cemetery. The afternoon grows hotter and hotter. I tell myself I must be crazy to be here. I would leave if I only knew the way home. . . .

Another dream: this time she is in my arms. We are sitting on stairs. The stairs are carpeted and comfortable. They may be the same stairs on which I sat so often with my wife before she was my wife, but I'm not sure.

She is sitting on my lap, her back to me. She moves her hips counterclockwise, slowly, keeps moving them as we talk and keeps me in a state of excitement and knows she is keeping me hard. My hands are cupped over her breasts under her blouse as we talk, and as we talk I am thinking to myself it is pleasant to have an erection but that I will not be able to have an orgasm, that somehow there will not be time. She turns her face around toward me. She is very pretty, streaks of blond hair falling over the left side of her face as she rides and swivels on my lap. I lean back, uncup my hands from her in a gesture of, perhaps, disdain. Why didn't you do this when we had time? I ask her. I didn't know how, she says. She smiles, and closes her eyes, and bites her lower lip, and leans back into me until I awake. . . .

I am walking with my son, who is half my son and half Henry, my youngest brother, who is the same age in this dream and in my life now as Henry was when I used to watch over him, play with him, take care of him. There are many photos of Henry and me playing ball one summer under the pear trees of our back lawn in Nesconset, and under the great cherry of an autumn with the tree above us reaching its bare branches into the Long Island sky for twenty years now, that still sky, the same sky under which we are now, my half-son half-brother and I, walking across Terlik's field, but at evening, dusk, too dark for faces, walking toward the house and barns. Harmonica music from a distance, maybe an accordion playing, sweet rasping sounds, low chords, and laughter rising above the music, shouts. Then I notice strings of colored bulbs in the trees behind the

106

house, crepe ribbons twined in the branches, people's shadows. Billy, who is just Billy now, and I stop in the center of the field in the darkness in the damp grass and listen to the noises coming out of the trees and watch the colored lights and shadows behind Terlik's house. Then we are standing inside somewhere, inside a barn, what used to be a barn but is now polished and shined. It is, in fact, almost elegant inside, the timbers rough, but silks hung all over, and I should not be there because I haven't shaved and I am wearing baggy pants and my old ski hat pulled down over my ears, and we are standing at a street corner in the barn in a crowd, the sound of chimes and small bells coming toward us from the left. I realize we are at a wedding.

Four horses come into view, round the corner where we are standing. Chimes and small bells, a throaty humming as though the chimes and bells were accompanied by a harmonica or an accordion. Or it is the background of one of the Shirelles' records. Four horses, a magnificent carriage, cheers from the faceless crowd for the driver. The driver of the carriage is the groom. He is wearing a silk hat and tails and is reining the horses around that corner perfectly, the left-front horse just grazing its left ear on the barn wall. Cheers, applause, the sound of bells. They are very rich, I am thinking. I strain to see the bride. Yes, I am thinking, she must be very rich. The groom is reining the horses, guiding them around that corner perfectly. My only thought about the bride is that she must be very rich. If, inside that dream last night, I saw her and recognized her, I cannot recall even a glimpse of her now. Nor am I sure whether or not I was the groom. A split second after the profile of the driver of that carriage

passed us, Billy and I were walking back home, our backs to
the colored lights strung out like eyes in Terlik's trees.

XXIII

From John Woolman's *Journal* (1774): "Then returned to
the island, where I spent the remainder of the week May,
1756 in visiting meetings. The Lord, I believe, hath a people
in those parts who are honestly inclined to serve Him; but
many I fear, are too much clogged with the things of this life,
and do not come forward bearing the cross in such faithful-
ness as He calls for."

William Oliver Stevens (1939): "The little white church
at Smithtown Branch is not much more than one hundred
years old, but, like that other church in Huntington, its
predecessor on this site had a hard experience during the
Revolutionary War. The preacher, Joshua Hart, was so fear-
less in the way he denounced the behavior of the British
troops that one soldier took a shot at him from the pews, but
fortunately missed. It is one of those rare cases in history when
some member of a congregation has dared to answer back the
man in the pulpit, but he might have done it more decorously
than with a musket."

From Wallace Stevens's *Journal* (Jan. 4, 1907): "There is
so little in reality. My office is dingy, and I go to and from
it, underground.—But sometimes I get glimpses of Washing-
ton Bridge and its neighborhood, and I think it all very im-
pressive and Roman and wonderful, in its way.—And on
Sundays I take walks here and there: one, lately, through
Yonkers Park, Scarsdale, along Weaver-Street to New-

Rochelle, and then down Pelham Road to Bartow. Twilight clings to the shores of the Sound like mist to a wood. There is no country here. That's one trouble.—"

Lois J. Watt (1963): "The Indian hunters' footprints disappeared and the wood from their arrows deteriorated through the hundreds of years since they lived here. At least we have their 'arrowhead footprints,' positive evidence that they once walked and hunted on the shores of Lake Ronkonkoma." Martha B. Flint (1896): "The Indians had a most superstitious reverence for Ronkonkoma. They even refused to catch the fish thronging its clear waters, believing them under the special protection of the Great Spirit, while on its beaches were held the most solemn of their ceremonies." F. W. Hodge (1885): "Offerings were made to beings in lakes, rivers, springs, except that in such cases poles were placed at the edge of the water. Dogs were hung on trees or tall poles."

From a letter to Lord Howe, Commander of the British forces in North America, published in *Pennsylvania Evening Post* (Sept. 7, 1776): "Let your lordship select ten thousand of your best troops and officers, with your lordship at their head; draw them up on the extensive plains of Long Island, where you will have every opportunity of displaying your great abilities. Arrange them in whatever manner you please; then let an equal number of Americans form themselves in battalia, and let each army be provided in all respects equal, with trains of artillery, and all other offensive weapons; then, on a given signal, begin the attack, and leave the issue to the God of armies. This is what the Americans propose to Lord Howe; and the sooner he agrees to the proposal the better."

Walt Whitman (1882): "As I write, the whole experience comes back to me after the lapse of forty and more years—

the soothing rustle of the waves, and the saline smell—boy-hood's times, the clam digging, barefoot, and with trousers roll'd up—hauling down the creek—the perfume of the sedge meadows—the hay boat, and the chowder fishing excursions."

XXIV

This is Gibbs Pond. I know this from the rise of the woods behind it. But it is very different. It is perfectly round now, and I can see through clear water to a sand bottom. The whole pond is only three or four feet deep, its whole bottom is sand. Not a single weed, no mud, not a branch or a log, just the clear water and yellow sand. I am wearing my bathing suit. I wade into the pond up to my waist. I have a snorkel and flippers. I submerge into what seems to be bright yellow water and swim languidly to the center of the pond. I touch the sand. It seems pasty. The water is very warm. It occurs to me that the water is unhealthy, and I am careful not to swallow any of it. At that moment I know that it is a terrible thing that has happened to Gibbs Pond. The water is much too warm. But I have no historical sense of what has happened to it.

At the center of the pond is a big round metal swimming pool. I reach it and stand up beside it and look inside. The water inside the swimming pool is brackish, and most of the water's surface is a tangle of lily pads and weeds. It is all that is left of the old pond. I touch the water inside. It is cool. A perch rises to my fingers as though to bits of bread. It is only about six inches long. It is banded gray and black, and I can just make out the red-orange tinge of its gills.

I can see, a few feet away, a painted turtle rising from far down. The turtle hovers just under a pad, its nostrils break the surface of the water at the notch where a stem is joined to its pad. As always before, the turtle's set of inner, cloudy lids is down over its eyes, but not the outer lids as it drinks air. The milky lids, I've always thought, give turtles an expression of obliviousness. The turtle drawing in the air above its small pond has the expression that my daughter had as my wife nursed her. My daughter's eyes would seem to be covered by a film. She often seemed to be dreaming. She often fell asleep while nursing. Without a ripple, the turtle descends again from where it had surfaced for air. I love that turtle. I picture its long claws curving into the bottom mud as it rakes for worms. It must be a female, I tell myself.

I am in the warm water of the outer pond up to my waist. The water is very uncomfortable. It smells, too. But the water does not carry the rich fragrance of mud or dead fish or lilies. The water smells of chemicals, peroxide and ammonia. I am very hot now, and I am getting dizzy. I am under the water swimming for shore again. Why is it always noon here? I ask myself this question again and again.

XXV (A letter to Vince Clemente, from Before I Knew Him)

May 28, 1973. Vince, you have some sense of what I've been up to. I thought that if I could write this to you, I could manage to get some things said without straining so much to be understood. Self-consciousness is murder. Enough.

I'm back on the Island for a week for a last look at the home and grounds and town where I grew up. My folks have sold out and are moving to a small house in a retirement community further east, about twenty-five miles from here. The property just got to be too much for them to take care of. The new owner and his wife dropped over yesterday evening. Nice people. He grew up in Franklin Square when it was country. I took him around the property and pointed out the stump of that magnificent cherry tree, and told him what the woods were like and where my father's shop used to be. He's a tile contractor, but I had him touch the bark of one of the last of the old apple trees. I took him under the grape arbor that is now completely undergrown with maples and weeds and black-eyed Susans and the spike stems of tiger lily that will bloom in late summer. I showed him the hundreds of dogwoods crowding the edge of the property. (I read somewhere that the English soaked the bark of these trees in water and used the mixture to wash down stinking dogs.) Some of the ones under the edges of the pine trees have been cut by the power mower so often that they now come up like bonsai—thick and small and old. Those pines behind the hedges along Gibbs Pond Road are at least seventy feet high now. Show trees, and still healthy and growing. The catalpa trees along one side of the driveway are all dead or dying—"like walking wounded," as Wilbur says about those lilacs. But between them other trees are young and flourishing. There are more birds here now than I ever remember. Even crows, which were never around when I was a kid. You know what this means. My father said he shot two of them out of the big linden last week.

Tonight I walked up the road past Zauzin's to Nesconset School. I stood foolishly in the moonlight and thought about the cornerstone and the day in 1949 when a newspaper was sealed into it, and my brother Ed's ball, and my brother

112

Henry's rattle. I read a speech that day—I think the speech is in the cornerstone, too—about all the improvements over the old school. I must have already learned to exaggerate by then, because I distinctly recall someone coming up to me later to say that I'd been wrong in saying that the windows of the old school had been dirty. Anyway, I began the sixth grade in that building. The teacher was a Mr. John White, a warm man. It's odd, but I remember so much about that year. I remember things Mr. White said in class, and what we studied, and where I sat. I remember that year almost week by week. Mr. White had been on the boxing team at Yale, and he cuffed us around often, but we knew he cared for us. I suppose he became another kind of father for me.

I walked over to the Nesconset firehouse, too. There's a commemorative slab of cement on the lawn that honors the veterans of this volunteer department who are dead. I remember so many of them—Abe Cohen, Tony and Louis Vion, old man McManus, Henry Dorfer—I remember their faces and manners. They always seemed to be over there at the department, shining the trucks or manning the booths at the annual carnival or running their clambakes and bingo parties. They were all *characters*. I spent a lot of time over there because I was a bugler with their drum and bugle outfit. I was a good one, too. Lots of wind. We practiced on the school field. The majorette was Claudette Cohen, Abe's daughter. She was an absolutely beautiful girl, blond as buttercups, friendly, a terrific figure, tall, leggy. A guy one class ahead of Werner's married her later on. His name was Buddy Fisher, and he must have been the envy of dozens of his friends. I mean she was a sweet girl, too. I heard about ten years ago that she was dying of cancer. And she did die. Then I heard that her father committed suicide. It all came back in a rush tonight. All those men whose names are on the slab are their own stories. I wish I could tell them. Is there nothing in our lives that can slow things down, can stop things for even a little while? I want to be able to turn the faces of those men in my mind and cherish them. Vince, have you seen the new Wright poem in which he realizes that he has become one of those old men? This is serious business, as Berryman would say. It will seem like ten minutes from now when you and I will be among the old guys. The older I get, the more amazing and astounding and astonishing and miraculous this life is. How is this consciousness of ours possible? How can we possibly exist as we do? And just what *is* this blur and depth that we call time? Lord, Lord, it all comes back to You.

So I am seeing this house for a last time and helping my parents move out—a twenty-six-year accumulation of *things*. Box after box after box. The wealth of America pouring out of every closet, drawer, cabinet. I'm taking back to Brockport with me a bowl and a creamer that belonged to my father's grandmother, a couple of pieces of crystal my mother got from an old woman when we lived in Woodhaven, and a few other nice things. I don't want to give the wrong impression. My folks are not rich and the house is not filled with antiques and crystal. But it is filled up. Leslie Fiedler says in an essay that there's only one thing for sale in America, and that's the Dream of many guises. The Dream comes disguised as Things. But what can we expect, he asks tenderly, of the culturally deprived and the dispossessed who came to America from all those tired lands? Things. Oh, and my folks have actually bought all these awful things that I've been helping to pack and move! The whole house is one knickknack shelf of glass and false gold and gaudy jeweled sequined shelled grotesque ornaments, tall plastic plants with exotic plastic birds. Immigrants. I've seen this phantasmagoric display so often with immigrants, the tractor tires painted white on the lawns of Italians in Lake Ronkonkoma and Kings Park, pink flamingos in the sand inside the tires and false brick tar paper on the porches and colored cement blocks along the walks.

I packed up all the stuff on the shelves over my father's bar. The liquor and wine went yesterday. Today was left the incredible variety of gimcrackery and gimmicks that surrounds the essential loneliness of alcohol. I packed boxes of cheap steins with false pewter lids. I packed my father's dodo-bird that dips its beak into water forever. I packed statuettes of drunks with red bulb noses, and glasses with false bottoms, and lucite ice cubes in which flies are embedded, and glasses with real rocks glued to their bottoms and "You asked for one on the rocks" printed on their sides. There were spouts of peeing boys and swizzle sticks with peephole girlie shows and coasters to cradle your drink between rubber tits. God knows what to make of all that stuff. My parents owned a bar in Hollis and then one in Happague before they moved to Nesconset and my father went back to carpentry, his trade from the Old Country. He now knows five hundred jokes about drunks and treasures his collection of alcoholiana. God knows what to make of it. Anything for a conversation. Maybe this is what he learned after ten years of tending bar.

I am finding out about things here, Vince. How is it that this acre or two of ground can mean so much to me? I'm a happy man! Then why does my mind skip back to the two maples, the three dogwoods, the pines along the road here, the single blue spruce hidden in deep shade? I'll be driving or walking along or talking over the phone and suddenly one or two of those particular trees flash into my mind. Vince, there's a perfect sentence, and a lead, in Seager's biography of Roethke. Listen: "The first definitions, the fruits of the primary glances, can never be supplanted, for the trees of one's childhood are the touchstones of all later trees, the grass of the back yard the measure of all greenness, and other lights fail because they are not the true sun that brightens those trees, that grass." Words fail me. An unbelievably fine poem is that sentence. And think of that line in Roethke's "The Far Field": "The pure serene of memory in one man."

I'll leave here tomorrow, then, for the last time. I will probably never return to Nesconset, or even to Smithtown. How can this be? Brockport *must* become my home now. I must allow it to become my home completely. This is important, and I'm sometimes afraid. What will resolve all of this? It really *is* a melodrama. Partial denouement: Mrs. Terlik, surviving her husband by twenty years now, plans to sell out and move to the city to live with her son and family. Wenzel is in the hospital and seems to be dying of stomach cancer. My father said he dreamed last night that he found Mrs. Wenzel dead in the front hedges. The wood my father sold next door is now a development of dozens of houses, and as Mrs. Terlik and Mrs. Wenzel and the Zauzins sell out, the development will spread. I've not gotten to St. James, and don't plan to. I suppose that her old man's barberpole, like the styles of hair these days, goes around and around and around.

XXVI

Our son is only a month or two old as I see the three of us, now, in the center of a scene the edges of which are smoke. The scene moves closer now, or I, the eye with which I see this, move closer. In this dream my wife and I are bending over our baby boy. He is on his back, on a blue bath towel, the towel tucked warmly around him, wisps of steam rising from his body into the air of this room: the back shed of a farmhouse I have somehow known. Old cupboards and a head-high cast-iron stove are presences in the background.

It is after his bath, and we are drying him, and I am burying my nose in the sweet-scented flesh of his neck. The three of us are happy. His little hands swim the air like minnows, his legs are drawn up like a frog's, as they were when he was this young. The corners of his mouth bubble. I can circle the whole girth of his chest with my two hands. I touch his nipples tenderly, run my hands smoothly over his belly. I notice his penis is straight and hard now, important twig of boyflesh, bud waiting to bloom. I touch him softly, the sacks of his testicles, his little penis. I notice he is still now, his blue eyes gazing dreamily into the clouds of white haze at the edges of the room. I touch him, his small bud wanting to flower. He exhales a hum, as when he is nursing, from deep in his throat, contented.

A bubble of his mother's milk appears on his lips, and now, as she and I look down, one pearl drop of his semen glistens, a drop of dew, a single frog's egg. His eyes close, but blue glows through his lids and lashes. He is asleep now, our boy. We are still bent over him, wrapping him in his blue towel. Though I see us from somewhere else, I know how I feel in this dream. These are our bodies, I say to myself. This is the peace that is possible in our lives. This is our love. Our son's eyes glow blue through his lids as he sleeps.

XXVII

I am with Billy, my son. We are clamming at St. James Harbor. I am crippled, but doing the best I can in the low water. I have used a board to scrape away layers of sand, and I am down now like a crab, feeling for clams with my hands. I hope to help my son fill two or three bushels before the tide is too high, but I am crippled. In this dream Billy is strong, muscles rippling his back as he bears down on his rake. He seems to be about fifteen, and is filling his basket, but I want to help, but I am crippled, but I strike a pocket, begin pulling as many clams out of the sand as my hands can stretch to hold.
 . . . Look at this, I shout to my son.

He wades over, the blue water lapping his knees. I am still pulling clams by the half-dozen from the pocket. Then one clamshell splits open. There is a mother-of-pearl box inside. Inside the box is an unsigned letter. The letter says, *We left these here for you.*

XXVIII

It was a May afternoon in 1957, my senior year in high school. I was at home, shooting baskets by myself up against the old woodshed where a rim was mounted, when my mother called me to the phone. It was Karen. She said that there had been a terrible accident on the Smithtown Bypass. She was crying. She said that Ellen Vallone and Bob Andrews had been driving around after school and that there had been an accident, that Ellen was actually dead. I went outside again and began shooting baskets again, but dizzily and in a kind of frenzy. My mother called me to the phone again. Karen sobbed, Oh God, that Bob was dead, too. I couldn't believe it, and thought there was a chance I was dreaming.

I went to Bob's funeral, saw his cosmetized face and hands in the casket, my first such experience. I made it through that. But Ellen was a Catholic, and our whole class attended a mass for her. I'd never been inside a Catholic church before. The crucifix, incense, the Latin and dark strangeness, frightened me and broke me down completely. I wept, right there in the presence of my friends, who also wept.

It is four in the morning now. Just a little while ago, seventeen years later, I dreamed I boarded a bus and walked down its aisle, its tunnel, to the back. Outside its windows, a starry blackness streamed by.

I first tried to squeeze into a seat in front, but it was too close, there were too many people. I was uncomfortable and moved to the back. Then there was an argument behind me—a friend of mine was involved with a tall man dressed in a black suit, a man handsome as Valentino. He was with a woman. She was wearing a beige veil. I looked back at her and then away and then back at her. She saw me.

. . . Is it you, Bill? she asked.

. . . Is it you, Ellen?

She has gotten older, is my age now, but is still beautiful, wearing her auburn hair short as she always wore it, her teeth perfect as always.

I lifted her shadowy veil. We embraced, and because we both now realized the truth about so much that had once frightened us, cried, and because we knew one another, the altercation between her escort and my friend turned into a handshake. Ellen and I embraced for a long time. . . .

XXIX

We'd moved from Woodhaven (which was anything but wooded) to the wilds of Happauge when I was four or five, and then to Nesconset where I began third grade. "O world so far away! O my lost world!" says Roethke. But he knew, at the same time, that the lost world would always live inside him.

Later, by school bus, or riding with my parents, or hitchhiking to high school on New York Avenue, I would pass through Smithtown Branch, under the great locusts, beside the Blydenburgh house. The one-room Smithtown schoolhouse where Whitman taught is just off the Jericho in the area across from the old Presbyterian Church where 25A begins its winding to St. James and Stony Brook, and 111 right-angles left to Happauge. You can see it from the Jericho. Last I knew, it housed a lawyer's office. When I think of Smithtown, I first think of that place, that confluence. I understand that our word "nostalgia" comes from two Greek words for pain and for a return home.

I didn't know anything about Whitman. When I remember myself as I was, I picture a boy wading Gibbs Pond in Nesconset or the nearby salt waters, the natural world bending in. I spent so much time in the water that this is the most enduring image I have of myself, and now I know that Whitman saw me, and now I know that the *presence* I felt when I was otherwise alone at a pond or walking through woods or, later, clamming at St. James Harbor, was his, as he is abiding spirit, as he is the miraculous confluence of space and time within a human voice.

Writing my poem "The Traffic," I was thinking of that busiest block of Bull Smith's town. My speaker, "Trying to leave Smithtown," is stuck in traffic, "here, where Whitman trooped / to tally the eighth-month flowers' bloom." He is dizzied by a truck's fumes, and falls back into the past world of this same place:

> *Lilacs utter their heart-shaped leaves,*
> *locusts spell their shade.   The Jericho's air*
> *creaks with cartwheels, a carriage*
> *moves with the certainty of mirage.*
>
> *The Widow Blydenburgh flows to church,*
> *stoops to admire an iris, and to smell.*
> *A pigeon bends the slim branch of a birch.*
> *The Widow plucks the iris for her Bible.*

But a truck's horn blares him back to the present. At the end of the poem, his head clear again, he glances to his right:

> and time's itself again.
> Pressed against the porch of Whitman's school,
> the dairy freeze is booming, winks
> its windows tinted green, and cool.

What is the true traffic? I am far from this poem now. It is as much any reader's as mine, as I try to hear it.

The irony seems heavy, and intended, but I wonder if I was writing more than I knew. Earlier in the poem the speaker had compared a truck's exhaust pipe to a "swan's neck," and now, it seems to me, the dairy freeze windows, "green, and cool," remind him bitterly of that other world of ponds that we know is a part of his sensibility. But I wonder if the poem, with its lines juxtaposing Whitman's school and the dairy freeze pressed against it, isn't more, doesn't, somehow, find a kind of solace in the present traffic, doesn't, somehow, trust the "booming" future as Whitman did. I notice, now, the cop's concern, the healing influence of the speaker's vision of the past, his humor, the blood-like *body* of the experience ("Red lights pulse and weave in"). I see now that "Glass sparkles," and now know—I don't know if I did when I wrote the poem— Whitman's "Sparkles from a Wheel" "Where the city's ceaseless crowd moves on the livelong day" with "Myself effusing and fluid, a phantom curiously floating. . . ." On Island ground, having been everywhere, part of the traffic river flowing up against Whitman's world, my speaker may be curiously at home with himself and his Island.

Just northeast of the confluence I've described is/was an estate of 37 acres, the Rockwell estate. Bull Smith obtained the land three centuries ago by Indian deed, and it was passed down through nine generations to Charles Embree Rockwell, 61 as of June 12, 1978, the date of a *Newsday* article sent me by a friend.

Unable to afford twentieth-century property taxes, Rockwell

sold 26 acres to The Point of Woods Construction Co. of Massapequa. He donated 1½ acres to the Town of Smithtown. And then he signed a contract of purchase for the remaining 9½ acres with Gordon and Jack Real Estate and Developers of Huntington. He plans to leave Long Island.

Rockwell once came into my father's woodworking shop on the Jericho with a walnut log from one of his trees fallen in a storm. Rockwell loved his trees, my father told me. He could tell this by the man's eyes and voice. Rockwell wanted to know what could be made out of the walnut log. It turned out that there were hollow spaces in its heartwood, but my father pieced together enough of it for a table pedestal.

Rockwell's son Charles, asked how he felt when he was told that the land had been sold, said, "Well, it's as if I had been told someone in the family had died."

I don't know the details of what is happening/will happen to that land. The two-story family house, built about 1750, is on the plot donated to the town. Near it is a large red barn built in 1850, and next to it a carriage house where "rows of cobwebbed carriages lie under decaying white dust covers." The *Newsday* article says that the town plans to move the family house but that the Smithtown Historical Society is against it, maintaining that its original site is the town's most important. Widow Blydenburgh's tavern stood on this land, too, and it was here that George Washington, on April 21, 1790, stopped to feed his horses and to thank Island residents for their support during the Revolution. The town may build a parking lot for the town library, if the Rockwell home is moved. Says Town Historian Virginia Malone, "I consider that to turn into a blacktop parking lot the place where the first president of the United States once greeted the residents of Smithtown, would be a desecration of the land."

The story goes/will go on and on. Its repetition across America does not make it any easier to understand. No one knows what it means, not Rockwell or the Town Historian or any number of lawyers in Whitman's school—"Were you looking to be held together by lawyers?" the poet once asked. "Nay, nor the world, nor any living thing, will so cohere." But as the maples, elms, walnut, oak, locust, hickory are lost, the blackberry brambles and honeysuckle and laurel, the dogwoods and lilac and wild roses, the deer and smaller animals, those of us in the traffic flow in the intersections of new and old Island bear witness with the center of our lives. There is no answer. I am not sure of the question. But we will come away from the Island with what we need for eternity. Despite whatever deaths we suffer, there will be compensation, in our knowledge of Whitman and Whitman's light.

XXX

This is Brockport, New York. The college's Hartwell Hall is much the same shape, and is built into the same air, as was the Baptist College constructed here in 1834, and the larger State Normal and Training School, which opened in 1867. (For just a moment, I float into the inner-rings of a maple in front of the building: I hear what it heard when it was a sapling— voices, another century's wind, the brooks and small creeks that drained this village, cartwheels, the wingbeats of millions of pigeons in a viridescent cloud shadowing the six-acre campus.) Now I know it is almost morning, and I am close to awakening, but, yes, this is Hartwell Hall, and I am staring at its facade, which is dirty and cob-webbed as I have never before seen it, the legend *State Teachers College* above its center doors incised in stone as always, but now lined with grime.

I am passing through the basement of this building, walking to a class. Two or three women are clearing out an alcove in the east wing, and in the back of my mind is the knowledge that the building is being shut down and its contents sold off the way an old church that has lost its congregation will sell off its pews and silver and hymnals.

The women have uncovered some things there in the dust of the alcove under papers and behind a pair of unhinged doors. They've brought out candle molds, a pleater, two circular stained-glass windows, a posthole digger, Normal School textbooks, old amber bottles, and a wicker planter with copper lining that needs only a spray of white paint to be worth fifty bucks. And they have placed on a window ledge another small object. I pick it up and skim the dust from it with my right thumb.

It is a trapezoid of glass. It is a small cowbell, not metal as is every other cowbell I have ever seen, but blown from blue glass, the pontil on its crown. Its small clapper hangs inside its dome like a single perfect grape. It is, as I weigh it in my hands, the most beautiful piece of glass I have ever seen, and it is marked 1940. The date stands out clearly. I hold the bell up to my eyes, and look through it, and the building's long lower hall is bathed in blue light.

It is urgent that I talk to one of the women and ask the price of the cowbell. Fifteen dollars, she says, and says that all these things will be brought over to another building to be sold. If only I had that much money. I begin to leave, but think of my wife, who would want to have the glass bell for our china cabinet, and then I check my left pocket and see that I have more than enough money, a whole fistful of fives and tens and singles. I return to the woman and ask her if I can buy the bell now, please. No, she says, you can never buy it, but you can be the first one on the list. All right, I say, and ask her, please, to be sure.

I cradle the glass bell in my hands. It holds my childhood, holds Long Island's light forever. All the way to morning I know that I will always have it with me when I need it.

XXXI

During my grammar school years I had seven or eight aquariums filled with tropical fish. I remember a list I once made of fifty-six different kinds I had collected, bicycling back and forth to Guarini's Pet Shop on the Jericho Turnpike, exchanging weeks of my allowance for a pair of pencil fish (though it was almost impossible with any egg-laying fish to tell male from female) or blind caves or gouramis. All these tanks were in an alcove behind the living-room couch where I would spend my evenings, especially in winter when I missed the Nesconset ponds, maybe glancing over at the twelve-inch black-and-white television set we had, but usually staring into an aquarium.

I didn't like ornaments, the bridges, galleons, divers my friends had in their tanks—a few weeks and these things looked algae-sick. And I knew that the lime in sea-shells dissolved to kill freshwater fish. I liked only gravel, enough plants for the livebearers' fry to hide in, and the fish themselves. But there was still a lot of color and glitter in those tanks, shine of neon tetras and rosy barbs, the mica-flecked hatchets, the bright orange swordtails.

This morning, in this other life, twenty-five years and the width of New York State away from that one, I was downstairs looking out a window at birds scratching in the snow a few feet away. Low drifts had covered the sunflower seeds I'd thrown there, and juncos and sparrows were getting down to them. I was daydreaming, remembering hundreds of chicks warming themselves around a stove in one of Wenzel's sheds, remembering that they scratched instinctively, even if the grain were spread on a sheet of tin.

A pair of cardinals has stayed close this winter. I see them about once a week, along the woodline in back. They appeared there this morning, in the ash-brush, and then, as I hoped they would, flew into the midst of the other birds in front of me.

The male cardinal is a shocking splash of red, brilliant and striking. It is amazing that nature can distill and hold this color within a world of snow and brown sparrows and gray-white juncos and brown woods. The male is a phenomenon, but the female is, to my eye, the most beautiful, her body in this morning's light a gift, a luminous silver-gray, only her tail, wingtips, and crest touched red.

I watched her this morning, remembered, and received with another eye the fish I most loved. I had only one. Guarini had received it as a stray in a batch of guppies, and had given it to me. We didn't know what kind of fish it was, but I realize now that it must have been a female. Her body was a luminous silver-gray, and only the edges of her fins were touched red.

XXXII

Jack and his wife Gail live a few houses down the street. He is self-employed, an electrician, and works hard. Gail is not well, usually stays inside, and when in company talks incessantly and loudly as though a moment's silence would wound. Their only son, Chuck, was nineteen when he was killed in Viet Nam in the Mekong Delta in 1969. They were the first ones on the block, as the song from *Woodstock* went, to have their son come home in a box. Jack has been in a daze ever since, rushing from job to job in his green pickup, but always distracted. I have seen him have to force himself to attention three times to change a light-switch. All of us along this street sense great pain and unhappiness emanating from their home. We pray that Jack and Gail will be all right, in the end, after a time, somehow.

Jack has kept up everything at his place, paints at least one side of the house every summer, mows his lawn, washes his pickup. But there's an in-ground swimming pool in their back yard they haven't used or taken care of for five years. One of its cement sides caved in a couple of winters ago because he didn't drain the pool or throw some logs in, and the water has been black-green with mud and algae.

Last summer my son and the other neighborhood boys who fish for bass, carp, suckers, catfish, and perch up at the Erie Canal, got the idea of bringing their catch home and dumping it into the unused pool. Jack told them he didn't mind. Every couple of days the boys dumped in a bucket of fish. I walked over there once to watch the fish-shadows sail up into the shallow end and disappear again into the depths of what had once been this suburban swimming pool. In the evenings, from our back porch, I could see across our yards to Jack sitting beside his pool. He'd throw bread to the fish and stare down into the murky water. The neighborhood boys didn't bother Jack on summer evenings. Even at night, I'd see his silhouette over there, leaning over the pool. Sometimes, by moonlight, he must have seen his own face in the water. Sometimes, the black water must have seemed to be his body.

We all wondered, of course, if any fish could survive the winter in a pool only eight feet deep at the deep end. I didn't know why not, I told my son, but didn't know about a food supply or about how much mud they might need at the bottom.

Now it is January and the pool is frozen. This morning I walked across the snow to Jack's yard where my son and his friends had cut holes in the pool's ice and were fishing with worms one of the boys had frozen in his parents' freezer for just this occasion. The water was very dark under its sky of ice.

And the fish were biting! I could see the poles snap down. In those seconds I remembered ice-fishing at Gibbs Pond from the hood of a Model-A rusting in the water when I was a boy.

I saw Jack watching the fishing from a back window. I waved to him, but he seemed not to see me. I waited around for a while to see if one of the boys could land a fish, but it seems that Jack had told them to file the barbs from their hooks.

At dinner this evening my son said that one of the boys had managed to bring up a perch. Jack was outside then as the fish flapped on the ice. He grabbed it quickly and slipped it back into a hole and looked down through that hole, my son said, for a long time. Then Jack said, "That's right, Chuck. Make

sure you throw them all back. That's the way. You got to make
sure you throw them all back."

XXXIII

Mid-November after three days of rain, sleet, winds that took
a couple of shingles from the roof. Today the sun came out
for the afternoon and I rushed to clean out the garage for
winter, backed the car, moved the bicycles, lawnmower, wheel-
barrow, got things onto shelves and into the garbage cans, and
swept the cement. An apple had rolled into a corner and
scented it to ripe sweetness. Are apples the only flesh that rots
with such a constant delicious smell?

I gathered some flower bulbs that hadn't been planted, and
wrapped them into newspapers for the spring. I was about
done when I found a coffee can on a ladder-rung. It was half-
filled with dirt, something we never waste here in suburbia. I
thought I'd empty it onto the front lawn, maybe under our
flowering mountain ash, now leafless, its bunches of orange
berries ready for the grackles, the only birds that seem to want
them.

When I emptied the can a ball of worms rolled out onto the
lawn, a glistening fist of mucus, night-crawlers with their
darkly swollen sex segments, and smaller, very pink worms,
and a few worms white and apparently dead, the whole mass
not unlike a brain dripping ganglia, or intestines suddenly
shocked to find themselves in the sunlight and chill November
air. They lay sodden for a few moments, but then began to
move, the outer worms already sliding quickly away under the
grass, earth instinct, gravity, some dim and simple cellular

130

pleasure and necessity drawing them into the ground again. A half-hour later, they were gone, every one, even those I thought were dead, and every idea about them.

XXXIV

Sunrise. The Island is a cradle below me, and I am falling, without fear, slowing as I near the earth. Then I am there, a hundred yards from the sacred tree, walking toward it, but this time not along a tar road, but on a path, as it must have been, the tree's body a wall at the end of the path.

This is your Island, Island tree. This is your Island. What is the music in the air? I know it is made of leaves and the sun rising, of crickets and small animals, but this does not explain this world's melodic hum. In music, I walk the path descending toward the tree, as I have before, and will again, knowing even as I dream that my dream is dying. But what is the music in the air? . . .

My dream took me to a slight valley in Setauket, to Lubbers Oak, probably the Island's oldest living thing. A guidebook says that it dates back to the 1400's. Now, reaching into the 1980's, it is almost dead, its one living limb the only one not cut back fifteen or twenty feet above the ground.

It is a white oak. Its bark is smoky gray, and its remaining leaves have rounded lobes. I have never seen a tree as vulnerable, as darkly beautiful.

Much of its great base is rotted out now. When I last knelt there, I found inside it on the ground a smooth white stone as big as your skull. Maybe it came from the Sound, toward which its one living limb points. I don't know why someone

131

had placed the stone there. Maybe so that it would remind the dying tree that time was nothing.

I'll tell you a secret: I placed the white stone inside the tree. I hope you like it there. This is your Island.

XXXV

I am walking across Main Street in Brockport, the plant shop behind me, its windows filled with vines and wild beach roses that I can see with eyes at the back of my head. I am walking across to the movies. I know I am supposed to meet my wife and children when they come out.

A girl is standing at the curb where I am crossing. She is wearing a black rubber diving suit, and goggles. She is still dripping, having just surfaced. She holds out toward me in her right hand the shell of a chambered nautilus. For an instant, I am lost in its swirl.

. . . I got this down there, she says, pointing at the pavement with her left hand.

I am crossing the street. Under the traffic light, the blacktop has worn away. I can see the red bricks of the old street, and hundred-year-old rails embedded in the bricks. I close my eyes: I can see flatcars of America's first reapers, built in Brockport, traveling these rails toward the vanishing point of the prairies.

I am almost across the street. Water laps the exposed rails now, and almost reaches the top of the far curb. The water is pure, pale green and black-green, and restless, the ocean water I knew as a child. I can taste its salt on my lips.

Have I ever been this happy? I am glad about the plants filling the windows behind me. I am glad about the ocean water rising onto the Brockport sidewalks.

III

The Odor of Pear

No wind bends the branches of those trees
behind my eyes, way back past
any distance I've a name for.

Though tears begin to gather like the rain,
they cannot bend the leaves of those trees
behind my eyes, far back past

any distance I've a name for.
For I remember pears, globed
to rust and gold, that yellowjackets tunneled

to the end of heavy summer. They'll never
rot and fall: for now, once more,
for all my time, the deep

odor of pear drifts up
from any distance I've a name for.

The Lamb

Both hindlegs wrapped with rope,
Wenzel's chosen lamb hung head down
from a branch of one of his elms.

Its throat slashed, the lamb drained,
its nose and neckwool dripping,
lawn soaking up the bright blood.

Once skinned, once emptied of its blue
and yellow organs, its translucent
strings of intestines, and though its eyes

still bulged, the lamb rose
like steam from the pail of its guts,
toward stray shafts of sunlight

filtering through the trees. Until
it came to pass: I forgot my knees,
and entered the deep kingdom of death.

Cow, Willow, Skull, Cowbell

I

Gravity wants her.
Strings of spittle
drool from her slack jaw;
her coat hangs down in folds.
She just won't make it
for much longer.
Her knees
buckle,
the highest weeds tickle
tenderest her.

II

The earth draws nothing down to it
so much as a willow
or old cow.

There's a spell under a willow,
a magic circle, the space
behind a waterfall.

Should the cow enter there, double
her own power, poof,
she'd be gone.

III

You'd think the rain, by now,
would have washed its edges smooth,
but the skull is chipped sharp.

You'd think, once it wore to pure bone,
insects would have nothing to do with it,

but it's always an ant's mountain,
a butterfly's throne.

Boss's shell dreams of water:
her meadow stretches away, like sand;
grass sways in the waves of the wind.

IV

A cowbell,
high up in one of the oaks
at the edge of Wenzel's meadow,
is brushed by leaves falling
like fingernails.

Whoever slung it over
a sapling's limb
is gone,
the skulls of its cows
are beyond hearing,

but if Wenzel has his way,
this bell will ring
with a silver tongue
when the dead break grass again.

The resurrection may begin
this windy autumn.

Providence

Knowledge as sure to him as his name:
Bradford knows, as he looks back,
that God deflected the Indians' first arrows,
that God's "sweet and gentle showers"
spared the corn, that God's voice
echoed as though from a dream
to save the burning storehouse.
How could they otherwise have lived,
these, the chosen?—
eleven heads of households,
four wives, six young men, a handful
of children still alive at Governor William's
first of thirty elections.
These would descend to the land,
to fifty-pound pumpkins
to heft to their shoulders,
to whole trotlines of bullheads
pulled from the terrible swift rivers,
to turkeys with six-foot wingspreads,
to the myriad shellfish of the shores.

The cruel sailor who cursed them:
the first struck down
and pitched over the side.
Proof. How else could Samoset have risen
from the woods to speak to them in English?
Evidence. Knowledge as certain
as God's people, here, in His land,

where they would *live,*
and be useful with their backs,
and look up to the Lord of the Air
for sunlight when they needed sunlight
to pray by. They all knew,
and this knowledge never
splintered off from a man,
or cut him in half,
or got lost angling to nowhere. The immediate
odor of a rose, of Sharon's Rose:
succor this sweet, knowledge this sure.
O, Father, as he writes,
the Governor's body blossoms only with Thee.

Witness

We'd walked into the small warm shed
where spring lambs lay in straw
in the half-dark still smelling of their birth,
of ammonia, the damp grass, dung,
into this world in the middle of a field
where lambs bleating soft songs lifted
their too-heavy heads toward their mothers,
gentle presences within their wool clouds.
Later, outside, as I watched,
Wenzel wrapped his left arm around a sheep's neck
and struck her with the sledge in his right hand.
The dying sheep, her forehead crushed, cried out,
past pain, for her mortal life.   Blood flowed
from her burst skull, over her eyes, her black nose.
Wenzel dropped her to the grass.
When I ran home, I struck my head
on a blossoming apple-bough.
Where was the dead sheep?
What did I hear?
Where is the witness now?

I was nine or ten.
Her cry was terror,
so I lay awake to hear her,
to wonder why she didn't seem to know
her next manger, her golden fields.
Her odors drifted through my screen—
the hay at the roots of her wool,

her urine, the wet graindust under her chin,
her birth fluids hot and flecked with blood.
I could hear her bleat
to her last lamb, hear her heartbeat
in the black air of my room.
Where was the dead sheep?
Why did she cry for her loss?
Where is the witness now?

Not to accept, but to awaken.
Not to understand, to cry terror, but to know
that even a billion years later, now,
we breathe the first circle of light,
and the light curves into us, into the deer's back,
the man's neck, the woman's thigh,
the cat's mouse-mossed tongue, all the ruby
berries ripening in evening air.
The dead elms and chestnuts are of it, and do not
break the curve. The jeweled flies sip it,
and do not break the curve.
Our homes inhabit, and ride the curve.
The mountains, its children, do not break the curve.
Our moon, our rivers, the furthest stars blinking blue,
the great named and nameless comets do not break the curve.
The odorous apple-blossom rain does not break the curve.
The struck ewe's broken brainpan does not break the curve.
Wenzel nor this witness breaks the curve.

In the shed's dusk where spring lambs
sang to their mothers, in my dark room
where the dead ewe's odors drifted my sleep,

143

and now, within these cells where her forehead blood
flows once more into recollection,
the light curves.   You and I bear witness, and know this,
and as we do the light curves into this knowledge.
The struck ewe lives in this light,
in this curve of the only unbroken light.

The Ewe

Ropes to her hind legs and the elm's branch
held her just above the ground in silhouette.
I'd almost run into her, but veered away in time,
and now knelt out of range
of her bulbous eyes, her cavernous ribcage.

I was alone, stared, and the dead ewe,
plane of silver flesh and flesh-shadowed bone
flamed into light, flew downward into the ground,
and disappeared.   When, from this other world,
she rose into silhouette again,

I crawled closer, as I remember,
looked up into her eyes, and entered. . . .
And last night, kneeling within a dream
under her eyes again, I entered, and here,
in this cave of silence, at the poised

center of being, in the ewe's skull,
I received her light, but the human
power of color, the sunset lavenders,
the moon-silvered meadow,
the curved sledge burst with stars.

A Tour on the Prairies

"I found my ravenous and sanguinary propensities
daily growing stronger upon the prairies,"
said Irving, as though between
sniffs of snuff.

But he was right, of course. After the Romantic, after
disports of melancholy suffused with redolence
of "moss-grown skulls of deer,"
or a hillside where

"long herbage was pressed down with numerous elk beds,"
after the picturesque, the Creeks' "well-turned
thighs and legs," their "Gypsy fondness
for brilliant colors,"

after the "fine Roman countenance of the Osage,"
and the Delawares' eagle god whose
miraculous feathers "render
the wearer invisible,"

after repast of "venison, fresh killed, roasted, or broiled,
on the coals, turkeys just from the thickets
and wild honey from the trees,"
after meat eaten

from "tapering spits of dogwood," after coffee "boiled
and sweetened with brown sugar, and drunk
from tin cups," after
a pinch of sorrow

for a dying buffalo or bear tracked to the end of its blood,
after a civilized shudder at vultures
banking in blue thermals
above him,

occurred what he called a "relapse," a regression
to the basic prose of man's "instinct
for destruction." A saddlebag
of tongues jounced

on his mount's rump as he rode. What could he, whose Hudson
flowed a world of German spells, make of this,
this *prairie* where a "man
may become

bewildered, and lose his way as readily as in the wastes
of the ocean?" Now it was October,
and the "waning year" sent
streams of wild geese

across the skies. "A distant flock of pelicans stalked
like spectres about a shallow pool." He woke
"to the sinister croaking of a raven
in the air." October: now

the rain ran off into deep pits his horse shied from,
or leapt over, and when it did, Irving, hunter,
looked down into mirrors that kept
giving him back to himself.

Man of the Sea

Not to believe in him
   is to call the old men rocking
      in caned chairs on the docks liars.

He rises, there, close enough:
   eyes lidded yellow,
      hair matted fur and seaweed.

Not a porpoise shredded past recognition.
   More like a man, but gill slits
      on the sides of his neck, his chest

an iridescence of scales. Seems
   to walk in water. Rips holes
      in fishnets, drags whole strings

of eelpots out to sea.
   And he is old, and never sleeps, or sleeps
      lower than light. You'll never

sail upon him basking, full-length, like a shark,
   in the sun. Never try to hook him:
      hooks pass through him. Never try

to bring him down with a bullet:
   he was not meant to die.

Mermaid

Yesterday evening after gentle rain
the creature swam up out of the harbor.
On Main, in front of the movies,
she lay gazing up at the early stars
with human eyes with gray lashes
and a far-off love-dream under her pupils.
Her hair still held the curve of a wave.

Most who left the movies hurried home,
but one man turned her over with his foot,
and watched, as another
knelt down to her
as though to kiss,
but cut a letter, *M*,
into her breast by razor.

Reports say an after-rain haze
lifted from sidewalk into the warm air,
but I was there: her blood was warm, the color
of blue water, circled her waist,
and smoked softly.   Twilight
received her.   This morning, only mist remains
of her blue trail back to the harbor.

The Swan

The sun reached pond's edge, past false
lily of the valley smoldering
in deep shade,

past oaks scrawled with vines
dripping the ink tears
of wild grape,

reached to the end of a path lined with thistles,
to a cove defined by cattails, to kindle
the corpse of a swan:

whose bill was a tiger lily,
whose eyes burned blind
to the rising sun.

Wind rose to lift its quills, to fan
the white flames of its wings.
Dark water floated

the swan's neck, now curved limp
as a snake's shed skin.
I breathed

the pond's pollen, studied the water's haze
where spiders and sprites walked,
bugs swam circles,

pads curled their edges. At noon,
mud swirled and flowered,
the pond towed

the swan away: that said nothing, nothing
but the black light that flared
from its eyes as it sailed.

The Snapper

He is the pond's old father, its brain
and dark, permanent presence.

He is the snapper, and smells
rich and sick as a mat of weeds; and wears

a beard of leeches that suck frog, fish,
and snake blood from his neck; and drags

a tail ridged as though hacked out
with an ax. He rises: mud swirls

and blooms, lilies bob, water washes
his moss-humped back where, buried

deep in his sweet flesh, the pond ebbs
and flows its sure, slow heart.

Candling

Maybe an egg in ten,
held over a hole in the lighted box,
balanced a spot of blood
that glowed softly through its shell.

Maybe an egg in a thousand
floated what seemed to be
a curve of white muscle,
a web of soft bones,

an eye like a sunflower seed.
These were the bad eggs,
unfit for puddings or cakes.
Wenzel said it takes

all kinds to make a world,
it takes all kinds.

Pet's Death

A truck crept
into our driveway,
but caught him
in its rear wheels.

We buried him
under the twin maples
in our back yard.
Let this be a lesson,

my father said,
but for nights I heard
my dog clawing his way out until,
one morning, his grave

was sunken.
But it was only rain
during the night,
my father said, and threw down

a few shovels of dirt.
But I continued
to dream him:
he was dirty and wet,

but he slept
as he slept in his shed,
curled in his corner
like a possum.

The Cat

I

Patched
in the shade and sunlight

of morning, I knelt
in the wood's silence,

gunstock against
my cheek, fired again, again.

Soon
the cat's skull, lapped

by snails, became
a spider's kingdom, a bowl

of shade darker
than the oaks', under which,

among sweet honeysuckle, ferns,
brambles that scratched my blood to surface,

the cat had crawled,
dragging its disobedient body,

trailing splashes
of blood, but will not die.

II

This is the deep field
I leveled in my sights and held

tight to a cross:
rabbits that leapt and died in midair

in the meadows' light:
a coon whose spine snapped like a stick

when my bullet hit;
watersnakes whose black, shining backs

fell headless from pads to pondwater;
the trophy buck I tracked to where

he raked his dark rack on birchbark, but fell
to his knees on the wood's floor,

his breath spraying the black moss and gold
needles with blood;

the starlings, their feathers scattering
as the birdshot struck.

III

Now, at dusk, summer and winter,
when cats' eyes catch

my carlights, drift away to haunt
the dark brush,

I, too, rush toward the dead.
For nothing we do

is lost. The skulls of bear,
deer,

cats glow white as hot coals
in the woods. This

is the mystics' luminous darkness.
Light strikes and steers

for far stars forever, beasts' eyes
burn bodiless

in the heavens, and I will always
return, bearing with me

the dark light, the foxfire
of all my dead.

Cat and Star

(It takes nearly five hundred years for light from
the North Star to reach the earth. If we were on
that star with a powerful telescope, we would be
able to see Columbus's ships just now arriving in the
New World. Nothing we do is ever lost to light.)

I

Dusk,
and the first white star,
white Polaris, drifts
the wide sky.
So,

it comes to everything,
again,
and again: the same
lilies of the valley
tremble

their white bells,
ferns of whip-
slender stems
duck their intricate
triangular heads

below my knees,
the same oaks rise
from the roots

of their own shadows.
And somewhere ahead, past

drops of precious berry-red
on the brush, the cat
still drags its broken body
over the last twenty years'
leaves.

II

So be it, it
is done again:

the cat—one eye
weeping blood,

the other a luster of dead
pearl light steering,

forever, a signal,
to a star—

adjusts its rust fur
to the wind,

draws its claws back inside
the pads of its paws,

settles its body
to the soft ground.

159

But here, now,
the sound of the cat crying

with all the dead light
of its dead eye.

III

In moments like this,
my whole life draws toward me
as though through water,

or tears, and rays
of the earth's light, and waves
of the earth's sound, redolence

of pear, paradisiacal
honeysuckle, moss, all
that Island's air until

the same summer morning,
the pealing white bells of lily,
those nodding fronds of fern,

those woods
and that cat, until,
once more, it is time

to kneel, to hear
the spatter of rifle fire,
and the cat's last retched snarls.

IV

I believe in the light
that still travels to somewhere,
objective light,
the cat and boy together.

I believe in the light,
and there may be a star
in the outer dark or
behind my eyes, where

the light turns back again,
the spider unravels its web
from the cat's skull,
the snails spit back

the cat's brains,
the honeysuckle sips its fumes
from diffuse summer,
the cat's entrails

build back cell by cell
from a broil of maggots:
I rise from my knees
and the red cat

twists up from the leaves,
its walleye jells, clears
to a shine, hardens
to a black lacquer,

the sun falls
over the Island's east edge,
and I am back in bed,
never to begin this,

my rifle in its closet,
the cat's eyes green slashes
of the lively firefly
and cricket-perfect night.

V

It goes on, this long story, this melodrama
about a kid who shot a cat.

It goes on until it touches the laws
of weight and grace, until

even that same summer morning's same
delicate ferns arc back

to exactly where and when they balanced
their heads in air

before I walked there. It goes on until it reaches
the laws of light, until

I no longer need to be struck by a hammer to name
this twenty-year obsession, this life's

redemption, this evidence, this instance,
this radiance for what it is.

Dusk

I have climbed
in present tense again
the branch-ladder nailed

into the oak-trunk: the shop-built
nest's roof lifts
open on a hinge:

wavery low
satin flames
glow from the bottom,

from sprinkles of bones
and two small skulls
alive in their own dead light.

The Return

I will touch things and things
and no more thoughts.
—Robinson Jeffers

My boat slowed on the still water,
stopped in a thatch of lilies.
The moon leaned over the white lilies.

I waited for a sign, and stared
at the hooded water. On the far shore
brush broke, a deer broke cover.

I waited for a sign, and waited.
The moon lit the lilies to candles.
Their light reached down the water

to a dark flame, a fish: it hovered
under the pads, the pond held it
in its dim depths as though in amber.

Green, still, balanced in its own life,
breathing small breaths of light, this
was the world's oldest wonder, the arrow

of thought, the branch that all words
break against, the deep fire, the pure poise
of an object, the pond's presence, the pike.

Oak Autumn

Strict
as dry brush or
a steel engraving of
reeds, cattails, cracked
pods, it is pure
of limb, lifts blades
of lines, is limned
of cuts, this
oak of one windless
instant of late
autumn, only
sun in its branches, not
a gauze or shimmer or
web of sunlight but
sun that etches bark to black
shine, only
spare branches sharp
in the air, austere
trunk, no
sky, no
horizon to mention, an un-
remarkable brown
field over which
the rise of this
uncluttered
life.

Oak Spring

Does not resist
its own leaves. These
appear, as easily as
snow, when winter snows,
or rain, when the sky rains,
or all the birds
it is always blind to.
But this blossoming, this
fulfillment, this
green explosion
every year of even its old age,
this different dimension
of miracle: snow, rain, birds,
yes, but imagine
all the sap of your own
wooden body beginning
to warm, your skin
breaking to bud and leaf;
imagine, coming
to everything you are,
without second, or third, or fourth,
or fifth thoughts
that each time you utter
this language of tongues,
you're living closer
to your last spring.

Maple and Starlings

Over my head, a maple fills with starlings
against the evening sky.
I won't move, I won't speak.
The maple will hold them as long as it does.

In a few seconds, the maple rising above me blossomed
with starlings. Darker than evening, darker than leaves,
they flew from nowhere to here for the first time.
I knew maple and starlings for the first time.

This evening, the maple above me turned to starlings.
A few moments, and everything was over, nothing
changed. The starlings flew from nowhere they remember.
The maple stands for nothing in the evening air.

How long had it been evening?
As long as starlings' shadows
were blowing through the maples.
As long as leaves were flying.

Over my head, a maple fills with evening,
releases flows of starlings,
or receives them,
wherever they came from, wherever they're going.

The maple growing into the evening above me fills
with starlings. For a few seconds, it's been as though
I've not been here to say *maple*, and *starlings*.
For a few seconds, the evening has darkened with starlings.

Someone has been dreaming: maple, starlings,
an evening second by second being its own darkness.
A maple rising in the dark air. Starlings
from nowhere to nowhere. A maple. Starlings.

Four Songs

I

In my first song I found
a rabbit's body,
fallen to tufts of fur,
to flesh stippled with maggots
where the ground received it.
I closed my eyes:
he tumbled, again, in the thick vines
at meadow's edge,
cried a rabbit's cry,
died a rabbit's death,
but my song tried to raise him
from the dead:
O, rabbit, shed
your blue coil of flies and worms
and walk whole.
But I walked home instead,
empty as a bell.

II

In my second song I sang
as though the world were more than world,
the dead were never dead.
Three dogwoods blossomed,
died, and blossomed again.
I watched the body of a wren

flare and ruffle toward impossible flight
in the white sun.
At Gibbs Pond, the same spiders walked
on eyelash legs, the same bluegills
fanned their same nests in the same sands
year after year.
O, Lord of eternal cricketsong, I come
to mark even the fireflies
whose lives, through the thick dusk,
flash on and off and on
before my eyes.

III

Then I held my flesh over a flame,
smashed my bones against a wall,
called out his name,
cursed his desertion
into the long nights.
He didn't answer:
in my third song my father
lay as meaningless as stone.
And I went on alone, until,
one evening at St. James Harbor,
I reached the far shore of surrender.

IV

Lord of poised rocks
shimmering in moonshine,

Lord of matter, and more, Lord
of Being, Lord of myself and the deep notes
of tides, creatures, trees
tending toward me almost beyond hearing,
reciprocal Lord of nothing, and all,
Lord of abandon,
Lord of mica,
Lord of the harbor's shine and haze,
I lodge my fourth song
in the thin book of praise.

Wenzel

Locusts, too, always green
except their husks, sang shrill
from trees along Nesconset roads,
and yellowjackets tunnelled Wenzel's roosts,

and networks of rats in the same dark
that slept all day
to carry pullets away at night,
when the farmer did not waken,

when feathers swished along the rats' tunnels
where now Nesconset lives on small piles
of coins and bones.   But Wenzel died.   Only a few of us
hear in the wind of a new Ford whipping by

bewitched hens' wings beating underground,
breeze of cow's tail along its rump of flies,
an owl welcoming dark to the far pastures,
Wenzel humming inside the tires.

Brockport, New York: Beginning With "And"

And it is Friday, and August,
and now the traffic subsides
and the haze of roadside dust
disappears.   Our small lawn
darkens into evening.
A daddylonglegs ascends a dandelion stem
in effortless eyelash meters that anyone
would want to speak,
and the tiny firefly lanterns wink against
our red maples' blood-red black-red bodies.
The air, as air will, cools
and sweetens.

Our lives here in this port town
vanish, but slowly, but vanish.
Would it help to scream?   Would it help to leave?
Some neighbors' children have grown up,
some of the children's parents have died,
always to remain for them
in series of still, and fond, and boring poses
that will never alter, no matter
their children's ages or even should winds
savage as flames sweep our streets.

If it is true, as Li Po prayed it might be,
that ourselves and our shadows and the moon
will meet again in the Milky Way,
his "Cloudy River of the Sky,"

if it is true,
and if it is true. . . .

And toward the Thruway, in the shopping centers,
the package stores glow in lights the colors
of their own liquors, drugstores
in aspirin-white fluorescence.   Now
lines at the banks
thin out, a ton of paychecks
cashed and ready for sorting.   And.
And couples in the corners of the bars whisper
maybe sex, maybe cancer, maybe
the end of another summer.

We are looking out over the evening
where the years come from.   We talk,
saying the same things:
five Augusts more, or one, or forty,
now or later, we and/or/and
our friends will die, our children travel
to their own ends,
but someone, if we awaken into the old prayer,

as billions of grassblades lose their light,
as maples rise sable-red within the black air,
as years number us further and further away,
as stars course their patterns
and the earth flows Li Po's eternal river,
someone will know, and remember,
and be set dreaming,
and will say "and."

Refrain

If, as they say, I'll return,
altered, somehow,
to my moments of exultation,

feeling, somehow,
the ponds' deep prescience,
their sway and weight,

their millions of small lives,
their corridors of sunlight and shadow;
if, as they say, I'll return,

feeling my parents' hands on my shoulders,
feeling the blessings of brothers,
remembering children and the love of one woman;

if, as they say, I'll return,
bearing with me the brain of water,
the heart of the harbor of nothing and white light;

if I return, I'll bow, and the great cherry
in the distance in the wind in the deep field
will bow, and those I've loved

and been loved by will know, somehow,
that this is the same garden where
we've wanted to find ourselves, forever.

The River

When, in the end,
we came to the river,
I hoped to float our wagon.
I remember
someone crying for help.
I never found out,
but it was not my wife,
my son, or my daughter—they
were safe beside me.
I pictured a woman trapped
in the wooden spokes of a wheel, turning
under the water, turning
back up to the air
to cry for her life.
I could not find her to help her.
But our wagon floated,
and we four knelt down
on the far shore.

I can still see the horses
breasting the current, their
wet rumps shining, their
black blinders flashing
in the slant sun.
I can still see my daughter
wrapping her arms about her brother
as he wraps her shawl
about her shoulders.

I can still see my wife's bonnet
filling in the wind,
and our wagon's canvas
filling in the wind.
Shouldn't I have known?
Later, the red sun
set in its east for the first time.

I should have known.
My life had deepened like a valley
to hold the river.
All my years the maples
tried to tell me, and the jays
that burned in the pineboughs
like blue flames,
and the winter pears
that hardened and reddened in the wind.
I should have known
that we would pass to the river,
that our wagon would float across it,
that we would kneel in the rich earth
of this shore, in this
abiding dream, this
miracle that goes on and on, this
new life that will never
cease to nourish, or amaze.

Bus Trip

I

The dirty snow?
The sign that says *Pete's Meats*
above a back alley in Buffalo?
The roadsides' sharp brown thistles?
The plume of greasy smoke
trailing the diesel?
Lord of Being, what are these to me?

Reflectors studding the Thruway miles
with red eyes? The steel median,
and every concrete culvert?
The veteran's medals and ribbons?
The rusty silo rising outside the city?
The cornstalks threading the winter fields?
The frail white shell floating the winter sky?
The great pine fallen
in clouds of green across a fence?
The Rochester wino's worn heels?
Lord of Being, what are these to me?

II

The frozen pond appearing
over my left shoulder?—
I close my eyes:
its fish school under my lids under a crag
under the ice-flashed water.

The tent worms webbing
skeletal roadside oaks?—
I close my eyes:
I have burned them out of branches,
thousands falling like lit fuses to the grass.

The male ring-
necked pheasant's tail?—
I close my eyes:
along the brainfield, from the beginning,
brilliant feathers strewn on Locke's snow.

III

Lord, though that trip was years ago,
though that winter is another spring,
I still feel those wings.
Even now, in nests woven into the cynical
grainfields' creases and furrows, real
pheasants harden into being in their eggs,
and there is always time to touch them,
the females' overlapped bent beaks,
the red leathery feathers around the males' eyes.

The Circle

Early morning, walking
Brockport woods after a fresh snow,
I found a ten-foot circle
sprayed with blood, still
smoking. . . . Splayed track, the big toe
spreading wide from the back foot like a human
hand's thumb,
and the tail-track dragging,
named the victim: a possum.
Puddle of gore
near where its body was pinned down,
near which, single incision
burning black into the snow
in the morning light,
the X, the hooked cross,
talon scar of the great killer,
the horned owl.
I imagined
silent descent of wingspread
out of the trees, the victim's punctured
back, its severed spine,
and in its lightning-struck brain
nothing to save its children
the next time.

Son Dream

I went looking for my son
and found him in the grass,
prone, his chin in his hands,
watching a black bull snake.
I said, "Be careful, my son,
anything can happen."
Beside him, somehow, a possum
rolled from under leaves, bared its teeth,
but licked his ear.   I said
"Watch out."   At that
a coon appeared,
touched my son's nose
gently with its pink fingers,
and lay down beside him.
I stood in my tracks, afraid, until
a wolf rose from the grass,
and licked my son's forehead.
My heart pumped the word *rabid*
into the space behind my eyes.
"He is only twelve, Lord," I prayed.
The gun was soundless when I fired.
The snake, the animals
began to shine, to shine.
My son and I walked home, holding hands.
He said, "I love you,"
but when I looked back he lay in the grass,
his chin cupped in his hands,
the snake and animals a shining
circle around him.

Daughter Dream

If now my daughter,
there in her tree,
calls down to me,
"Father, try harder.
Father, don't leave me"—
if now my daughter
almost falls but rights herself
in air and glides away—
if now my daughter
is a white pigeon
circling above me,
her wings backlit, her
breastbone a cream-white curve in the sky—
if now she is this beautiful,
and I have failed her—
why shouldn't my eyes
fill with tears?
And just when I have lost her,
why shouldn't she, as she does,
alight beside me,
grow to my shoulder again,
become my daughter again,
and clasp my hands together in hers?
Why shouldn't she, as she does,
as she walks away again,
as my hands grow cold again,
why shouldn't my beautiful daughter ask,
"Father, why have you left me?
Father, why have you died?"

The Heart

Last night my daughter could not find her twins
in the bodiless heavens,
and cried.   Lord

of Being, the wheat rusts, children starve, the cities
bleed, You have never been so far away
for so long.   With your love

we could all root trees in our breastbone marrow.
Still, this morning, when its pale
green hands reached

to right-angle the darkness, I heard my wrist
watch beating its metal heart.
Your each second

is a wonder made from night, from nothing.
Each second the world's pulse
dies, buds again,

blooms rose-red, yellow, blue, green,
miraculous black.

The Carrie White Auction at Brockport, May 1974
(for Han)

We sit under the tall trees to wait.
The old woman—we didn't know her—her life
is lined up across the grass.   These things whisper.

Waking early some mornings we hear the bells
of the bridge of the old barge canal that brought this town,
board by board, and dime by dime.   Maybe
down the road there is talk, held low as we listen,
heard as though from the other world.

We know so much we never have to think of.
A dozen miles north,
just as it did when Carrie was a girl,
the great lake laps shore.   Storybook clouds sweep
south, white against blue sky.

The auctioneer holds up a mirror:
we are together now; we see ourselves in poses
only the light will always remember.
The trees disappear in a burst of glare. . . .

In the glass of her hand-blown bottle,
another century's air is caught in bubbles.
The bottle casts a blue-white shadow, now, on our table,

so perfect, so still.   She was ninety years old,
and lived here, only here, only here.

Trees, grass, sun, the rushing sky,
and an old woman we never knew.

There has not yet been an ending to this,
unless it is not true that some intention of her eyes
is still held in the bottle's blue
(she must have looked at it so often),
something of her touch in its wavy glass
(she must have held it so often).

The Crow

Snow crystals
swirl up from gravel
almost to beautiful white-out.
In the parking lot, high

in a lone tree over the store
in whose window diamonds
still break to blue-
white desire in my mind,

a crow,
black intricate jewel,
cries out for all my life
that I am still a fool.

The Language

In the center of Brockport,
above the banked rocks
along the Erie Canal,
on a wild grapevine's
largest leaf,
a young snake
coiled sleeping
in October sun.
I knelt near,
my skull's shadow
covering the leaf
and snake body blending
its symmetries of scales
green into the leaf.
When, as though I
were part of its sky,
it looked up,
lowered its head,
and slept again,
I closed my eyes,
hoping for the reptile's
attractive nothingness.
The snake's language,
of course, was wordless,
and I, as though this desire
were worth it,
as though the still
autumn water and vista

of yellow maples
demanded this oblivion,
began to drift
into the snake's sunburst brain,
until, for a few beats
of our hearts,
I joined it on its leaf.
But soon, as here,
dimension of the human,
the world became its words again,
the Main Street mutter
of traffic *traffic*, even
mica on a rock, *mica*.
I looked, in time,
to see the leaf tremble,
the snake's mission
to disappear
beneath the rocks,
mine to coil it,
as I do here,
tighter again, and tighter,
against its grapeleaf.

Fires

"*The prairies burning form some of the most beautiful scenes that are
to be witnessed in the country, and also some of the most sublime.*"
—George Catlin

I

Where, on prairie elevations,
   grass clings thin, sparse, as low
      as in what Easterners would call a meadow, no
animal fears the gentle fire it smells

from far away.   Sometimes invisible,
   the burn's feeble flame
      travels to the eye as only its black line,
and when they must, as they must each autumn

when lightning seems to strike off
   yellow sections of itself
      lateral across this land,
the wild bodies who know fire

will wait for it to tongue their lairs,
   will step over it or walk through it
      across the warm cinders
to another year.   At night, the flame's

luminous blue wavery liquid edge
    pours over the sides and tops
        of bluffs in chains, "hanging suspended,"
as George Catlin put it in 1830,

"in graceful festoons from the skies."
    With him, we could watch this nightfire
        for a long time: even the stars appear
to rise from ground that the sinuous

soft flame blackens behind it.
    With him, we could watch this nightfire
        for a long time, bed down
on the still-warm ground behind it,

and sleep, the waving
    flames receding
        in grasshead sparkles
like Andromeda, or a dream.

II

But Catlin knew that the place came
    for us to stand erect
        in our mounts' stirrups, to stare for fire
over the tall cover of flatland grass,

in other country, along the Missouri,
    the Platte, the Arkansas.
        To be caught here is to die:
pea-vines tangle the eight-foot grasses,

fire drives smoke before it, booms
    terror into the horses rearing up in circles:
        the leaping flames soon surround
to take all horsehair and flesh

in screams and thunderous noise.   We
    would not be the first.   Whole
        parties of Indians, herds
of buffalo and deer have burned into a charred meal

only ants are left alive to eat, and the roots
    of next spring's prairie.   These scenes
        roll with black smoke and streaks of red,
both beautiful and sublime, as the painter said.

III

Those galaxies, each at least one hundred
    billion bodies falling away from us,
        one hundred billion, ten to the eleventh power,
billions dead and invisible already—

that is the far darkness.   Planets
    burn out, turn, for all we know,
        into ice, or cold moons, if anything only an unseen
trace of fern or beings in fossil to prove perished fire,

but here, for now, on this earth,
    even for those creatures whose marrow
        boiled within their bones
and through whose ribs the prairie wind

tuned itself to its own truth,
    even for these the fires sear
        something else.   Just now, within this revery of him,
not knowing, as in all of Catlin's paintings,

how to end this, or where, of its own discord, it does,
    I looked up again out
        of my twentieth-century window
over my left shoulder:

Catlin's West is dead, yes, in its own way,
    but the same sun's unimaginable power drives suburban
        and miraculous through flowers banked
against these houses, flames the black-flecked slashed vivid

undiminished orange heads of tiger lily, and even the most
    domestic geranium along a front border
        bursts with spots of fire red
as the open mouths of horses trapped in that other world.

IV

If much of this is sad, this
    necessary "civilized
        wilderness"
our minds have made for us,

still the fires kindle and begin,
    somewhere beneath the breastbone,
        somehow under the lungs,
radiate from rooftops,

192

the sunlit concrete,
   brick, even the black
      macadam to abdomen and groin, begin,
in their last stages, to leap up

into the city, into the brain's
   nerves and grasses, out
      into the fingers' touch, even
into love.   Catlin's West is lost, except

we still feel these fires, by night
   a necklace blue as a glass snake in the heavens,
      by day as flickering sun
tongues its way along a walk, the flash of steel

smokestacks, or in lightning, or the rains'
   rolling fog, at sunset
      in the burnished clouds rising
over lines of trees rising

over lines of buildings still
   burning, outside, within,
      with wild and elemental meanings
from our living sun.

The Elm's Home

I

A dark sky blowing over
our backyard maples,
the air already cool,
Brockport begins its autumn.
My mower's drone and power
drift past the first leaves fallen
curled into red and yellow fists.
In a corner of lawn against
an old wire fence against the older woods,
a grove of mushrooms the kids
already hacked umbrellaless with golfclubs
rots into a mush of lumped columns,
pleats and fans.

These are the suburbs
where I loved that tree, our one elm.
Now, an inch under the loam,
its stump is a candle
of slow decay, lighting, above it,
thousands of perfect pearls
tiered like ant-eggs,
and these, by nature, growing so low
my mower's blades will never touch them.

II

My precious secrets come
to this, then?   Yes.
Stay away from them,
you careless bastards.

But listen: sometimes,
at night, kneeling
within a dream within
the elm's oval shadow,

I can look down
into my leg-bones,
into my own marrow
clustered with eggs,

small and perfect pearl
mushrooms
living for all my life.
I can look up

into the elm and hear each leaf
whisper in my own breath, *welcome
home, this is your home,
welcome home.*

III

Sun, shine through me,
  for I have lost my body,
    my old elm gone home
  to its earthly city, O
sun, shine through me.

IV

Downward leader flash track
driving: 1,000 miles per second;
inconceivable return track:
87,000 miles per second.

But if we could stop it with our eyes:
its central core, hotter and brighter
than the surface of the sun,
only a half-inch to an inch diameter;

its corona envelope, or glow discharge,
ten to twenty feet.   Lightning:
our eyeballs' branched after-image.   Lightning:
smell of ozone in the air,

pure stroke and electric numen.

V

Last night, heat
lightning branching
the blue-black sky,
alone on our back lawn,
when I closed my eyes for the right time,
when I knelt within the nimbus
where the elm I loved
lived for a hundred years,

when I touched the loam fill over the elm's stump,
its clusters of tiny noctilucent mushrooms,
I saw through them
into the ground, into the elm's dead
luminous roots, the branches of heaven
under the earth, this island home,
my lightning lord,
my home.